THE ETHICS OF
ABORTION

Contemporary Issues in Philosophy

Series Editors: Robert M. Baird
Stuart E. Rosenbaum

Other titles in this series:

Philosophy of Punishment
edited by Robert M. Baird
and Stuart E. Rosenbaum

Morality and the Law
edited by Robert M. Baird
and Stuart E. Rosenbaum

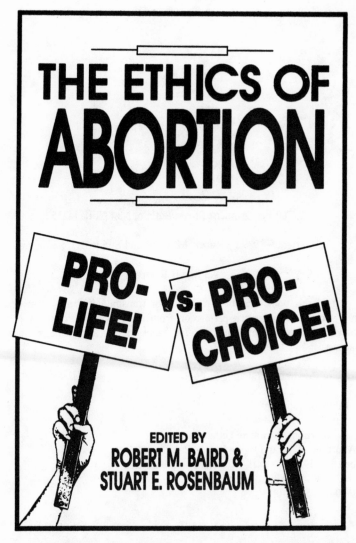

THE ETHICS OF ABORTION

PRO-LIFE! vs. PRO-CHOICE!

EDITED BY
**ROBERT M. BAIRD &
STUART E. ROSENBAUM**

CONTEMPORARY ISSUES IN PHILOSOPHY SERIES

71588

PROMETHEUS BOOKS
BUFFALO, NEW YORK

Published 1989 by Prometheus Books
700 East Amherst Street, Buffalo, New York 14215

Library of Congress Cataloging-in-Publication Data

The Ethics of abortion.

   1. Abortion—Moral and ethical aspects.
2. Abortion—Law and legislation. I. Baird,
Robert M., 1937–   . II. Rosenbaum, Stuart E.
HQ767.15.E84 1989   363.4'6   89-3549
ISBN 0-87975-521-0

Contents

6   Contents

Introduction

In *The Handmaid's Tale,* Margaret Atwood conceives a society of the future. Most readers of her book would regard that society as undesirable. Women hold positions of complete subservience to men, and function primarily to supply the society with healthy children. All social legitimacy for women derives from the biological role of mother; the duties of motherhood and household care (cooking, cleaning, and so on) are absolute. No woman may aspire to other roles.

Atwood's society is totalitarian, modelled after Orwell's *1984*. Spies are everywhere. Any "untoward" speech is reported to the authorities, who deal with it in a proper and punitive way. "Untoward" speech, of course, is speech suspected of being less than completely sympathetic to the rigidity of social structures, less than completely sympathetic to the subservient role of women, or less than passively accepting of limited possibilities for fulfillment. The spies are naturally rewarded with small tokens of appreciation for their support of the authorities. Consequently, women "squeal" on other women.

In this totalitarian, paternalistic society, abortion is unthinkable and unmentionable. Not only is each child needed for continuing the race, but the only legitimate goals for women are motherhood and household care. The penalty for abortion is death; the penalty for talking about abortion is death. Somewhat less severe penalties attend other rebellious offenses.

Atwood's imaginative construct is a totalitarian "anti-choice" society. Another example of such a society is found in contemporary Communist China. In recent years, official Chinese policy has allowed each nuclear family

to have only one child. Given China's enormous population and its astro-
nomical rate of increase, birth control is an understandable goal of Chinese
social policy. Once population growth begins to threaten social goals and
traditional institutions, policy concerns naturally focus on quality of life.
What social policies will enable the populace to continue at a minimally
adequate standard of living? Confronting such questions, Chinese policy
makers have agreed on the necessity of stabilizing the population. Among
the means they have chosen in their efforts to achieve the desired stability
can be found mandatory abortion for pregnant women who already have
one child. Standard birth control procedures are heavily emphasized, but
when failures occur, be they failures of the procedures themselves or lapses
of ideological commitment on the part of women who are required to use
them, abortion is mandated. Heavy pressure is brought to bear on women
to enforce the requirement of only one child per family.

Atwood's imagined society of the future and that of contemporary China
are very different: her society prohibits abortion, while Chinese society
mandates it. In spite of their great difference over the issue of abortion,
these two societies have much in common. Both devalue individual autonomy: choices are circumscribed within a very narrow range. In this respect,
they contrast dramatically with contemporary Western democracies.

One distinctive mark of modern Western democracies is their commitment to the view that as many decisions as possible about the shape of
individual lives should be left to the individuals who must live those lives.
In the matter of family size, for example, these democracies leave such decisions to their adult male and female members. Thus the social policies of
these democracies differ markedly from those of the Chinese. Again, in the
matter of a decision whether or not to have children, the democracies usually leave that decision to the women who would be responsible for their
care. Consequently, birth control is widely available and commonly prac-
ticed with care by most women of child-bearing age. Thus, the social policies of these democracies differ markedly from those of Atwood's imagi-
nary society.

A natural way to characterize the difference between democracies, on
one hand, and the totalitarian societies, on the other, is to say that the
democracies value individual autonomy and seek to maximize it when
possible. The totalitarian societies tend to devalue individual autonomy
because they are driven by moral and social goals that conflict with it.

The contrast between Atwood's society and that of the Communist
Chinese suggests different ways in which social policy may be marshalled
against individual autonomy. For the Chinese, traditional institutions, and
perhaps survival itself, are at stake in the choice to enforce rigid measures
against population growth. In this respect, the Chinese may be seen simply
as "hardheaded" realists, or perhaps as "pragmatists" in one common use

of the term. They may be trying as best they can to deal realistically with a virtually intractable social problem. On this way of understanding their enforcement of abortion on women who already have one child, the Chinese are just choosing the less undesirable of two undesirable alternatives. It is a common, if unfortunate, fact of life that such choices must frequently be made, by individuals as well as governments. Citizens of Western democracies may be properly grateful not to have been burdened as yet by the necessity of making such distressing choices.

In Atwood's society, individual autonomy is devalued, not for "pragmatic" reasons, but rather for ideological purposes. Her totalitarian society is structured by a religious ideology, according to which every human life is precious and every effort must be made to promote as much life as possible. Hence, the entire social structure is built around child-bearing and child-rearing. Women are sorted into two groups: those most likely to be able to give birth to healthy intelligent children, and those less likely. Women in the first group are required to submit to efforts to impregnate them by exemplary males. Women in the second group may not engage in any sexual activity. All such details are worked out by those competent to decide what social arrangements best accommodate the basic ideology.

The authoritarian character of these societies emerges from two different sources. For the Communist Chinese, it is the necessity of dealing efficiently and competently with an unfortunate reality. For Atwood's social planners, it is the necessity of finding the social arrangement most adequately expressive of fundamental religious commitments.

It is a mistake, of course, to see the pragmatic and the ideological motivations as mutually exclusive. Chinese social policy is driven by ideological components, and Atwood's social planners are moved by pragmatic considerations. The formulation of real policies is no doubt influenced by both kinds of motivations. Nevertheless, these are two different kinds of considerations that customarily give rise to the devaluing of individual autonomy.

In 1988, "Operation Rescue" was initiated during the Democratic National Convention in Atlanta, Georgia. "Operation Rescue" is the name of a movement among those of "pro-life"/anti-choice" sentiments aimed at saving unborn babies from abortion. Participants in "Operation Rescue" see abortion as nothing short of murder, the wanton and deliberate taking of innocent human life. Their tactics have included primarily conventional civil disobedience intended to disrupt provision of services at abortion clinics. Their commitment to this cause leads them to see analogies between the plight of unwanted unborn babies, Jews in Germany during the Second World War, and slaves in pre-Civil War America. Members of "Operation Rescue" think they see the same sort of moral myopia in the current practice of abortion that decent, enlightened people saw in the Germany of the thirties and forties and in the South prior to the Civil War. Since their commitment is primarily ideological, it has more in common with the commitments of Atwood's social planners than with those of the Communist Chinese. What can, or should, be done about such groups as "Operation Rescue," which are organized exclusively around strong ideological commitments?

This is a critical questions facing Western democracies at the end of the twentieth century. To what extent, and on what issues, should democracies compromise commitment to individual autonomy in an effort to realize other values, or to accommodate ideologies? This question becomes more pressing each year with a greater variety of issues. The quality of our environment, animal experimentation, AIDS testing, increasing numbers of aging adults, the plight of the homeless, and the rising death rate on our highways are only a few of the issues to which attention must be directed. The question for this volume is that of abortion.

Abortion is somewhat different from other issues about which this question of priorities arises. Many of these issues—quality of environment and the rising highway death rate, for example—are issues about which pragmatic considerations have largely dominated discussion; ideological considerations have not been prominent, because relevant ideological issues have yet to generate much division or conflict. Virtually everyone agrees that the highway death rate is much too high, and though some ways of trying to reduce it are a bit controversial—for example, the legally mandated wearing of seatbelts—a vast majority of citizens are willing to accept small intrusions on individual autonomy in order to make progress toward the social goal of reducing the death rate. In the case of abortion, however, ideological considerations have been most prominent. The vocal minority whose members agitate for the reversal of *Roe* v. *Wade* (the U.S. Supreme Court decision that legalized abortion) and picket abortion clinics do so because they subscribe to basic principles violated by the taking of human life before birth. Their objections do not derive from pragmatic considerations. Indeed, pragmatic considerations appear to tell against their view: uncontrolled growth of the human race has already produced such consequences as famine and disease that may in the future grow to disasterous proportions. "Pro-life" or "anti-choice" views about the abortion issue are primarily ideologically driven. In this respect the abortion issue differs from such issues as environmental quality and the highway death rate.

How should Western democracies deal with this issue, given their historic commitment to individual autonomy to whatever extent they deem it to be consistent with good social order? Since the motivation behind "pro-life" or "anti-choice" views is largely ideological, this question breaks naturally into two questions. The first is this: Is the ideologically motivated "pro-life"/"anti-choice" view solidly grounded in sources that enjoy pervasive respect among the people of Western democracies? Is it, for example, so deeply a part of Western moral tradition that allowing frequent choice against it by women who choose abortion is also allowing a fundamental attack on the integrity of our own moral tradition? Or is it, alternatively, so fundamental a part of Western religious culture that allowing frequent choice against it by women who choose abortion is also allowing a fundamental attack on our own religious culture, and consequently undermining our own cultural identity? If the answer to this question, in whatever form it may be posed, is affirmative, then there is a presumption in favor of the "pro-life"/"anti-choice" views, and all considerate persons must put what effort they can into the task of reinforcing—morally, socially, and legally—the now tattered fabric of Western cultural integrity.

A second question is this: In the face of serious disagreement about ideology, to what extent should a society allow social policy to be ideologically driven? This question becomes vitally important primarily in case the answer to the first question is negative. If the ideology motivating the "pro-life"/"anti-choice" view is not so pervasive that failure to incorporate it decisively into institutional structures of society results in an attack on the integrity of society, then is it reasonable to allow ideologically driven social or legal policy? In this case, do not pragmatic considerations become paramount? For the case of abortion, pragmatic considerations include questions about the likelihood of a dramatic increase in population; about the quality of life for women, families, and neighborhoods; about the ratio of persons in society who live "below the poverty line"; and about similar considerations. If the ideological question is not given an affirmative answer, then considerations such as these must bear the burden of responsibility for the formation of public policy.

In dealing with this second question, it may well be instructive to consider some precedents. In the twentieth century, for example, prohibition was an ideologically driven legal proscription against the use of alcohol. Prohibition failed as a social policy, largely because of pragmatic considerations— too many people wanted to drink; too great an increase in blackmarket crimes was needed to serve their desires; and there was injustice to those who wanted to drink but abstained out of respect for the law even when it required extraordinary virtue on their part but not on the part of those less circumspect. Society would do well to deliberate carefully before restricting individual autonomy to serve an ideologically motivated goal.

Pragmatic considerations relevant to careful deliberation about alternative abortion policies may not properly serve as the primary focus of controversy until the first question is given all the attention it certainly deserves. The first question—To what extent and on what issues democracies should compromise their commitment to individual autonomy?—focuses on something like "the soul" of Western culture. If current abortion practice subsidizes individual autonomy only at the cost of sacrificing crucial moral or religious tradition, then that cost may be too high. Until clarity is achieved about that issue, moving beyond it to pragmatic considerations would be rash.

The primary goal of the present volume is to canvas issues surrounding the first question in sufficiently comprehensive a way that a reasonably informed preliminary opinion may be formed. Every effort has been made to represent, fairly and amply, prominent or influential positions about the issue. Is the current practice of allowing women to choose for themselves how to deal with unwanted pregnancies a fundamental violation of the core of Western moral, religious, social, or intellectual traditions? Or does current practice fall comfortably and justifiably within the Western custom of respecting individual autonomy?

In delivering the majority opinion in the 1973 decision of the Supreme Court of the United States, Justice Blackmun argued that the practice of abortion does not transgress the moral or religious traditions of Western culture. The excerpt we have included from his opinion incorporates his discussion of this issue. Among selections included here, those tending against the general tenor of Blackmun's claim are those by Richard Selzer, Paul Ramsey, Harry J. Gensler, and Sidney Callahan. The readings that tend to favor Blackmun's analysis are from Judith Jarvis Thomson, Michael Tooley, Mary Ann Warren, Jane English, Charles Hartshorne, and Joan Callahan. The reader should note that several of the selections in this volume were written before the Supreme Court rendered its decision on abortion. These essays are included because, though a great deal has been written on both sides of the abortion debate, these early works are still thought to offer the most compelling arguments for their respective positions. In fact, it is still the case that individuals currently writing on the subject recognize the need to address the arguments made in them.

Two other points about content are worth mentioning here. The first is that this collection includes a section from Justice White's dissenting opinion. It is of special interest not because it contests Blackmun's finding about the moral or religious acceptability of abortion, but because it regrets that the majority decision removes the question of abortion from the legislative domain in which it might be more thoroughly debated. Our second point is that the volume concludes with a sermon about abortion by a Southern Baptist minister, Reverend Roger Paynter.

We believe there is balance and order to the selections we have made. Each deserves careful study and critical attention.

Roe v. Wade

The 1973 Supreme Court Decision
on State Abortion Laws

Mr. Justice Blackmum delivered the opinion of the Court. . . .

We forthwith acknowledge our awareness of the sensitive and emotional nature of the abortion controversy, of the vigorous opposing views, even among physicians, and of the deep and seemingly absolute convictions that the subject inspires. One's philosophy, one's experiences, one's exposure to the raw edges of human existence, one's religious training, one's attitudes toward life and family and their values, and the moral standards one establishes and seeks to observe, are all likely to influence and to color one's thinking and conclusions about abortion.

In addition, population growth, pollution, poverty, and racial overtones tend to complicate and not to simplify the problem.

Our task, of course, is to resolve the issue by constitutional measurement, free of emotion and of predilection. . . .

Jane Roe,[1] a single woman who was residing in Dallas County, Texas, instituted this federal action in March 1970 against the District Attorney of the county. She sought a declaratory judgment that the Texas criminal abortion statutes were unconstitutional on their face and an injunction restraining the defendant* from enforcing the statutes.

Roe alleged that she was unmarried and pregnant; that she wished to terminate her pregnancy by an abortion "performed by a competent, licensed physician, under safe, clinical conditions"; that she was unable to get a "legal" abortion in Texas because her life did not appear to be threatened by the continuation of the pregnancy; and that she could not afford to travel to

From *United States Reports,* Vol. 410, pp. 113-178. Cases adjudged in the U.S. Supreme Court during the October Term, 1972.

*Here, the State of Texas—Eds.

another jurisdiction in order to secure a legal abortion under safe conditions. She claimed that the Texas statutes were unconstitutionally vague and that they abridged her right of personal privacy, protected by the First, Fourth, Fifth, Ninth, and Fourteenth Amendments. By an amendment to her complaint Roe purported to sue "on behalf of herself and all other women" similarly situated. . . .

The principal thrust of appellant's* attack on the Texas statutes is that they improperly invade a right, said to be possessed by the pregnant woman, to choose to terminate her pregnancy. Appellant would discover this right in the concept of personal "liberty" embodied in the Fourteenth Amendment's Due Process Clause; or in personal, marital, familial, and sexual privacy said to be protected by the Bill of Rights. . . .

It perhaps is not generally appreciated that the restrictive criminal abortion laws in effect in a majority of States today are of relatively recent vintage. Those laws, generally proscribing abortion or its attempt at any time during pregnancy except when necessary to preserve the pregnant woman's life, are not of ancient or even of common-law origin. Instead, they derive from statutory changes effected, for the most part, in the latter half of the nineteenth century. . . .

It is undisputed that at common law, abortion performed *before* "quickening"—the first recognizable movement of the fetus *in utero,* appearing usually from the sixteenth to the eighteenth week of pregnancy—was not an indictable offense. . . .

Whether abortion of a *quick* fetus was a felony at common law, or even a lesser crime, is still disputed. . . . A recent review of the common-law precedents argues, however, that . . . even post-quickening abortion was never established as a common-law crime. . . .

It is thus apparent that at common law, at the time of the adoption of our Constitution, and throughout the major portion of the nineteenth century, abortion was viewed with less disfavor than under most American statutes currently in effect. Phrasing it another way, a woman enjoyed a substantially broader right to terminate a pregnancy than she does in most States today. At least with respect to the early stage of pregnancy, and very possibly without such a limitation, the opportunity to make this choice was present in this country well into the nineteenth century. Even later, the law continued for some time to treat less punitively an abortion procured in early pregnancy. . . .

Three reasons have been advanced to explain historically the enactment of criminal abortion laws in the nineteenth century and to justify their continued existence. It has been argued occasionally that these laws were the product of a Victorian social concern to discourage illicit sexual conduct.

---

*Roe's—Eds.

Texas, however, does not advance this justification in the present case, and it appears that no court or commentator has taken the argument seriously. . . .

A second reason is concerned with abortion as a medical procedure. When most criminal abortion laws were first enacted, the procedure was a hazardous one for the woman. This was particularly true prior to the development of antisepsis. Antiseptic techniques, of course, were based on discoveries by Lister, Pasteur, and others first announced in 1867, but were not generally accepted and employed until about the turn of the century. Abortion mortality was high. Even after 1900, and perhaps until as late as the development of antibiotics in the 1940s, standard modern techniques such as dilatation and curettage* were not nearly so safe as they are today. Thus, it has been argued that a State's real concern in enacting a criminal abortion law was to protect the pregnant woman, that is, to restrain her from submitting to a procedure that placed her life in serious jeopardy.

Modern medical techniques have altered this situation. Appellants and various *amici*† refer to medical data indicating that abortion in early pregnancy, that is, prior to the end of the first trimester, although not without its risk, is now relatively safe. Mortality rates for women undergoing early abortions, where the procedure is legal, appear to be as low as or lower than the rates for normal childbirth. Consequently, any interest of the State in protecting the woman from an inherently hazardous procedure, except when it would be equally dangerous for her to forgo it, has largely disappeared. Of course, important state interests in the areas of health and medical standards do remain. The State has a legitimate interest in seeing to it that abortion, like any other medical procedure, is performed under circumstances that insure maximum safety for the patient. This interest obviously extends at least to the performing physician and his staff, to the facilities involved, to the availability of after-care, and to adequate provision for any complication or emergency that might arise. The prevalence of high mortality rates at illegal "abortion mills" strengthens, rather than weakens, the State's interest in regulating the conditions under which abortions are performed. Moreover, the risk to the woman increases as her pregnancy continues. Thus, the State retains a definite interest in protecting the woman's own health and safety when an abortion is proposed at a late stage of pregnancy.

The third reason is the State's interest—some phrase it in terms of duty—in protecting prenatal life. Some of the argument for this justification rests on the theory that a new human life is present from the moment of conception. The State's interest and general obligation to protect life then extends, it is argued, to prenatal life. Only when the life of the pregnant mother herself is at stake, balanced against the life she carries within her, should the interest

---

*Expanding the opening of the uterus and detaching the fetus from the uterine wall.—Eds.

†Legal briefs submitted by parties viewing themselves as "friends of the Court." These are often designed to provide valuable background information.—Eds.

of the embryo or fetus not prevail. Logically, of course, a legitimate state interest in this area need not stand or fall on acceptance of the belief that life begins at conception or at some other point prior to live birth. In assessing the State's interest, recognition may be given to the less rigid claim that as long as at least *potential* life is involved, the State may assert interests beyond the protection of the pregnant woman alone.

Parties challenging state abortion laws have sharply disputed in some courts the contention that a purpose of these laws, when enacted, was to protect prenatal life. Pointing to the absence of legislative history to support the contention, they claim that most state laws were designed solely to protect the woman. Because medical advances have lessened this concern, at least with respect to abortion in early pregnancy, they argue that with respect to such abortions the laws can no longer be justified by any state interest. There is some scholarly support for this view of original purpose. The few state courts called upon to interpret their laws in the late nineteenth and early twentieth centuries did focus on the State's interest in protecting the woman's health rather than in preserving the embryo and fetus. . . .

The Constitution does not explicitly mention any right of privacy. In a line of decisions, however, going back perhaps as far as *Union Pacific R. Co.* v. *Botsford* (1891) . . . the Court has recognized that a right of personal privacy, or a guarantee of certain areas or zones of privacy, does exist under the Constitution. In varying contexts, the Court or individual Justices have, indeed, found at least the roots of that right in the First Amendment, . . . in the Fourth and Fifth Amendments, . . . in the Ninth Amendment, . . . or in the concept of liberty guaranteed by the first section of the Fourteenth Amendment. . . . These decisions make it clear that only personal rights that can be deemed "fundamental" or "implicit in the concept of ordered liberty" . . . are included in this guarantee of personal privacy. They also make it clear that the right has some extension to activities relating to marriage, . . . procreation, . . . contraception, . . . family relationships, . . . and child rearing and education. . . .

This right of privacy, whether it be founded in the Fourteenth Amendment's concept of personal liberty and restrictions upon state action, as we feel it is, or, as the District Court determined, in the Ninth Amendment's reservation of rights to the people, is broad enough to encompass a woman's decision whether or not to terminate her pregnancy. The detriment that the State would impose upon the pregnant woman by denying this choice altogether is apparent. Specific and direct harm medically diagnosable even in early pregnancy may be involved. Maternity, or additional offspring, may force upon the woman a distressful life and future. Psychological harm may be imminent. Mental and physical health may be taxed by child care. There is also the distress, for all concerned, associated with the unwanted child, and there is the problem of bringing a child into a family already unable, psychologically and otherwise, to care for it. In other cases, as in this one, the additional difficulties and continuing stigma of unwed motherhood may be involved. All these are factors the woman and her responsible physician necessarily consider in consultation.

On the basis of elements such as these, appellant and some *amici* argue that the woman's right is absolute and that she is entitled to terminate her pregnancy at whatever time, in whatever way, and for whatever reason she alone chooses. With this we do not agree. Appellant's arguments that Texas either has no valid interest at all in regulating the abortion decision, or no interest strong enough to support any limitation upon the woman's sole determination, are unpersuasive. The Court's decisions recognizing a right of privacy also acknowledge that some state regulation in areas protected by that right is appropriate. As noted above, a State may properly assert important interests in safeguarding health, in maintaining medical standards, and in protecting potential life. At some point in pregnancy, these respective interests become sufficiently compelling to sustain regulation of the factors that govern the abortion decision. The privacy right involved, therefore, cannot be said to be absolute. In fact, it is not clear to us that the claim asserted by some *amici* that one has an unlimited right to do with one's body as one pleases bears a close relationship to the right of privacy previously articulated in the Court's decisions. The Court has refused to recognize an unlimited right of this kind in the past. . . .

We, therefore, conclude that the right of personal privacy includes the abortion decision, but that this right is not unqualified and must be considered against important state interests in regulation.

We note that those federal and state courts that have recently considered abortion law challenges have reached the same conclusion. . . .

Although the results are divided, most of these courts have agreed that the right of privacy, however based, is broad enough to cover the abortion decision; that the right, nonetheless, is not absolute and is subject to some limitations; and that at some point the state interests as to protection of health, medical standards, and prenatal life, become dominant. We agree with this approach. . . .

The appellee* and certain *amici* argue that the fetus is a "person" within the language and meaning of the Fourteenth Amendment. In support of this, they outline at length and in detail the well-known facts of fetal development. If this suggestion of personhood is established, the appellant's† case, of course, collapses, for the fetus's right to life would then be guaranteed specifically by the Amendment. The appellant conceded as much on reargument. On the other hand, the appellee conceded on reargument that

---

*The State of Texas—Eds.
†Roe's—Eds.

no case could be cited that holds that a fetus is a person within the meaning of the Fourteenth Amendment.

The Constitution does not define "person" in so many words. Section 1 of the Fourteenth Amendment contains three references to "person." The first, in defining "citizens," speaks of "persons born or naturalized in the United States." The word also appears both in the Due Process Clause and in the Equal Protection Clause. "Person" is used in other places in the Constitution: in the listing of qualifications for Representatives and Senators, Art, I, § 2, cl. 2, and § 3, cl. 3; in the Apportionment Clause, Art. I, § 2, cl. 3; in the Migration and Importation provision, Art. I, § 9, cl. 1; in the Emolument Clause, Art. I, § 9, cl. 8; in the Electors provisions, Art. II, § 1, cl. 2, and the superseded cl. 3; in the provision outlining qualifications for the office of President, Art. II, § 1, cl. 5; in the Extradition provisions, Art. IV, § 2, cl. 2, and the superseded Fugitive Slave Clause 3; and in the Fifth, Twelfth, and Twenty-second Amendments as well as in §§ 2 and 3 of the Fourteenth Amendment. But in nearly all these instances, the use of the word is such that it has application only postnatally. None indicates, with any assurance, that it has any possible pre-natal application.

All this, together with our observation, *supra,** that throughout the major portion of the nineteenth century prevailing legal abortion practices were far freer than they are today, persuades us that the word "person," as used in the Fourteenth Amendment, does not include the unborn. . . .

We need not resolve the difficult question of when life begins. When those trained in the respective disciplines of medicine, philosophy, and theology are unable to arrive at any consensus, the judiciary, at this point in the development of man's knowledge, is not in a position to speculate as to the answer.

It should be sufficient to note briefly the wide divergence of thinking on this most sensitive and difficult question. There has always been strong support for the view that life does not begin until live birth. This was the belief of the Stoics. It appears to be the predominant, though not the unanimous, attitude of the Jewish faith. It may be taken to represent also the position of a large segment of the Protestant community, insofar as that can be ascertained; organized groups that have taken a formal position on the abortion issue have generally regarded abortion as a matter for the conscience of the individual and her family. As we have noted, the common law found greater significance in quickening. Physicians and their scientific colleagues have regarded that event with less interest and have tended to focus either upon conception, upon live birth, or upon the interim point at which the fetus becomes "viable," that is, potentially able to live outside

---

*Common reference term in legal briefs. It means "cited above"—Eds.

the mother's womb, albeit with artificial aid. Viability is usually placed at about seven months (28 weeks) but may occur earlier, even at 24 weeks. The Aristotelian theory of "mediate animation," that held sway throughout the Middle Ages and the Renaissance in Europe, continued to be official Roman Catholic dogma until the nineteenth century, despite opposition to this "ensoulment" theory from those in the Church who would recognize the existence of life from the moment of conception. The latter is now, of course, the official belief of the Catholic Church. As one brief *amicus* discloses, this is a view strongly held by many non-Catholics as well, and by many physicians. Substantial problems for precise definition of this view are posed, however, by new embryological data that purport to indicate that conception is a "process" over time, rather than an event, and by new medical techniques such as menstrual extraction, the "morning-after" pill, implantation of embryos, artifical insemination, and even artificial wombs.

In areas other than criminal abortion, the law has been reluctant to endorse any theory that life, as we recognize it, begins before live birth or to accord legal rights to the unborn except in narrowly defined situations and except when the rights are contingent upon live birth. For example, the traditional rule of tort law denied recovery for prenatal injuries even though the child was born alive. That rule has been changed in almost every jurisdiction. In most States, recovery is said to be permitted only if the fetus was viable, or at least quick, when the injuries were sustained, though few courts have squarely so held. In a recent development, generally opposed by the commentators, some States permit the parents of a stillborn child to maintain an action for wrongful death because of prenatal injuries. Such an action, however, would appear to be one to vindicate the parents' interest and is thus consistent with the view that the fetus, at most, represents only the potentiality of life. Similarly, unborn children have been recognized as acquiring rights or interests by way of inheritance or other devolution of property, and have been represented by guardians *ad litem.** Perfection of the interests involved, again, has generally been contingent upon live birth. In short, the unborn have never been recognized in the law as persons in the whole sense.

In view of all this, we do not agree that, by adopting one theory of life, Texas may override the rights of the pregnant woman that are at stake. We repeat, however, that the State does have an important and legitimate interest in preserving and protecting the health of the pregnant woman, whether she be a resident of the State or a nonresident who seeks medical consultation and treatment there, and that it has still *another* important and legitimate interest in protecting the potentiality of human life. These interests are separate and distinct. Each grows in substantiality as the woman

---

*For the duration of a legal proceeding.—Eds.

approaches term and, at a point during pregnancy, each becomes "compelling."

With respect to the State's important and legitimate interest in the health of the mother, the "compelling" point, in the light of present medical knowledge, is at approximately the end of the first trimester. This is so because of the now-established medical fact . . . that until the end of the first trimester mortality in abortion may be less than mortality in normal childbirth. It follows that, from and after this point, a State may regulate the abortion procedure to the extent that the regulation reasonably relates to the preservation and protection of maternal health. Examples of permissible state regulation in this area are requirements as to the qualifications of the person who is to perform the abortion; as to the licensure of that person; as to the facility in which the procedure is to be performed, that is, whether it must be a hospital or may be a clinic or some other place of less-than-hospital status; as to the licensing of the facility; and the like.

This means, on the other hand, that, for the period of pregnancy prior to this "compelling" point, the attending physician, in consultation with his patient, is free to determine, without regulation by the State, that, in his medical judgment, the patient's pregnancy should be terminated. If that decision is reached, the judgment may be effectuated by an abortion free of interference by the State.

With respect to the State's important and legitimate interest in potential life, the "compelling" point is at viability. This is so because the fetus then presumably has the capability of meaningful life outside the mother's womb. State regulation protective of fetal life after viability thus has both logical and biological justifications. If the State is interested in protecting fetal life after viability, it may go so far as to proscribe abortion during that period, except when it is necessary to preserve the life or health of the mother. . . .

To summarize and to repeat:

1. A state criminal abortion statute of the current Texas type, that excepts from criminality only a *life-saving* procedure on behalf of the mother, without regard to pregnancy state and without recognition of the other interests involved, is violative of the Due Process Clause of the Fourteenth Amendment.

(a) For the stage prior to approximately the end of the first trimester, the abortion decision and its effectuation must be left to the medical judgment of the pregnant woman's attending physician.

(b) For the stage subsequent to approximately the end of the first trimester, the State, in promoting its interest in the health of the mother, may, if it chooses, regulate the abortion procedure in ways that are reasonably related to maternal health.

(c) For the stage subsequent to viability, the State in promoting its interest in the potentiality of human life may, if it chooses, regulate, and even proscribe, abortion except where it is necessary, in appropriate medical judgment, for the preservation of the life or health of the mother.

* * *

The decision leaves the State free to place increasing restrictions on abortion as the period of pregnancy lengthens, so long as those restrictions are tailored to the recognized state interests. The decision vindicates the right of the physician to administer medical treatment according to his professional judgment up to the points where important state interests provide compelling justifications for intervention. Up to those points, the abortion decision in all its aspects is inherently, and primarily, a medical decision, and basic responsibility for it must rest with the physician. If an individual practitioner abuses the privilege of exercising proper medical judgment, the usual remedies, judicial and intra-professional, are available. . . .

Mr. Justice White, with whom Mr. Justice Rehnquist joins, dissenting.[2]

At the heart of the controversy in these cases are those recurring pregnancies that pose no danger whatsoever to the life or health of the mother but are, nevertheless, unwanted for any one or more of a variety of reasons—convenience, family planning, economics, dislike of children, the embarrassment of illegitimacy, etc. The common claim before us is that for any one of such reasons, or for no reason at all, and without asserting or claiming any threat to life or health, any woman is entitled to an abortion at her request if she is able to find a medical advisor willing to undertake the procedure.

The Court for the most part sustains this position: During the period prior to the time the fetus becomes viable, the Constitution of the United States values the convenience, whim, or caprice of the putative mother more than the life or potential life of the fetus; the Constitution, therefore, guarantees the right to an abortion as against any state law or policy seeking to protect the fetus from an abortion not prompted by more compelling reasons of the mother.

With all due respect, I dissent. I find nothing in the language or history of the Constitution to support the Court's judgment. The Court simply fashions and announces a new constitutional right for pregnant mothers and, with scarcely any reason or authority for its action, invests that right with sufficient substance to override most existing state abortion statutes. The upshot is that the people and the legislatures of the fifty States are constitutionally disentitled to weigh the relative importance of the continued existence and development of the fetus, on the one hand, against a spectrum of possible impacts on the mother, on the other hand. As an exercise of raw judicial power, the Court perhaps has authority to do what it does today; but in my view its judgment is an improvident and extravagant exercise of the power of judicial review that the Constitution extends to this Court.

The Court apparently values the convenience of the pregnant mother more than the continued existence and development of the life or potential life that she carries. Whether or not I might agree with that marshaling of values, I can in no event join the Court's judgment, because I find no constitutional warrant for imposing such an order of priorities on the people and legislatures of the States. In a sensitive area such as this, involving as it does issues over which reasonable men may easily and heatedly differ, I cannot accept the Court's exercise of its clear power of choice by interposing a constitutional barrier to state efforts to protect human life and by investing mothers and doctors with the constitutionally protected right to exterminate it. This issue, for the most part, should be left with the people and to the political processes the people have devised to govern their affairs.

It is my view, therefore, that the Texas statute is not constitutionally infirm because it denies abortions to those who seek to serve only their convenience rather than to protect their life or health. . . .

NOTES

1. The name is a pseudonym.

2. This dissent was written in response to the Supreme Court's decision in *Doe* v. *Bolton*, but it was explicitly stated by the authors that the dissenting statement also applied to *Roe* v. *Wade*.

Abortion

Richard Selzer

Horror, like bacteria, is everywhere. It blankets the earth, endlessly lapping to find that one unguarded entryway. As though narcotized, we walk beneath, upon, through it. Carelessly we touch the familiar infected linen, eat from the universal dish; we disdain isolation. We are like the newborn that carry immunity from their mothers' wombs. Exteriorized, we are wrapped in impermeable membranes that cannot be seen. Then one day, the defense is gone. And we awaken to horror.

In our city, garbage is collected early in the morning. Sometimes the bang of the cans and the grind of the truck awaken us before our time. We are resentful, mutter into our pillows, then go back to sleep. On the morning of August 6, 1975, the people of 73rd Street near Woodside Avenue do just that. When at last they rise from their beds, dress, eat breakfast and leave their houses for work, they have forgotten, if they had ever known, that the garbage truck had passed earlier that morning. The event has slipped into unmemory, like a dream.

They close their doors and descend to the pavement. It is midsummer. You measure the climate, decide how you feel in relation to the heat and the humidity. You walk toward the bus stop. Others, your neighbors, are waiting there. It is all so familiar. All at once you step on something soft. You feel it with your foot. Even through your shoe you have the sense of something unusual, something marked by a special "give." It is a foreignness upon the pavement. Instinct pulls your foot away in an awkward little movement. You look down, and you see . . . a tiny naked body, its arms and legs flung apart, its head thrown back, its mouth agape, its face serious.

23

A bird, you think, fallen from its nest. But there is no nest here on 73rd Street, no bird so big. It is rubber, then. A model, a . . . joke. Yes, that's it, a joke. And you bend to see. Because you must. And it is no joke. Such a gray softness can be but one thing. It is a baby, and dead. You cover your mouth, your eyes. You are fixed. Horror has found its chink and crawled in, and you will never be the same as you were. Years later you will step from a sidewalk to a lawn, and you will start at its softness, and think of that upon which you have just trod.

Now you look about; another man has seen it too. "My God," he whispers. Others come, people you have seen every day for years, and you hear them speak with strangely altered voices. "Look," they say, "it's a baby." There is a cry. "Here's another!" and "Another!" and "Another!" And you follow with your gaze the index fingers of your friends pointing from the huddle where you cluster. Yes, it is true! There *are* more of these . . . little carcasses upon the street. And for a moment you look up to see if all the unbaptized sinless are falling from Limbo.

Now the street is filling with people. There are police. They know what to do. They rope off the area, then stand guard over the enclosed space. They are controlled methodical, these young policemen. Servants, they do not reveal themselves to their public master; it would not be seemly. Yet I do see their pallor and the sweat that breaks upon the face of one, the way another bites the lining of his cheek and holds it thus. Ambulance attendants scoop up the bodies. They scan the street; none must be overlooked. What they place upon the litter amounts to little more than a dozen pounds of human flesh. They raise the litter, and slide it home inside the ambulance, and they drive away. You and your neighbors stand about in the street which is become for you a battlefield from which the newly slain have at last been bagged and tagged and dragged away. *But what shrapnel is this? By what explosion flung, these fragments that sink into the brain and fester there?* Whatever smell there is in this place becomes for you the stench of death. The people of 73rd Street do not then speak to each other. It is too soon for outrage, too late for blindness. It is the time of unresisted horror.

Later, at the police station, the investigation is brisk, conclusive. It is the hospital director speaking: ". . . fetuses accidentally got mixed up with the hospital rubbish . . . were picked up at approximately eight fifteen A.M. by a sanitation truck. Somehow, the plastic lab bag, labeled HAZARDOUS MATERIAL, fell off the back of the truck and broke open. No, it is not known how the fetuses got in the orange plastic bag labeled HAZARDOUS MATERIAL. It is a freak accident." The hospital director wants you to know that it is not an everyday occurrence. Once in a lifetime, he says. But you have seen it, and what are his words to you now?

He grows affable, familiar, tells you that, by mistake, the fetuses got mixed up with the other debris. (Yes, he says *other;* he says *debris.*) He has spent the entire day, he says, trying to figure out how it happened. He wants you to know that. Somehow it matters to him. He goes on:

Aborted fetuses that weigh one pound or less are incinerated. Those weighing over one pound are buried at a city cemetery. He says this. Now you see. It *is* orderly. It *is* sensible. The world is *not* mad. This is still a civilized society.

There is no more. You turn to leave. Outside on the street, men are talking things over, reassuring each other that the right thing is being done. But just this once, you know it isn't. You saw, and you know.

And you know, too, that the Street of the Dead Fetuses will be wherever you go. You are part of its history now, its legend. It has laid claim upon you so that you cannot entirely leave it—not ever.

I am a surgeon. I do not shrink from the particularities of sick flesh. Escaping blood, all the outpourings of disease—phlegm, pus, vomitus, even those occult meaty tumors that terrify—I see as blood, disease, phlegm, and so on. I touch them to destroy them. But I do not make symbols of them. I have seen, and I am used to seeing. Yet there are paths within the body that I have not taken, penetralia where I do not go. Nor is it lack of technique, limitation of knowledge that forbids me these ways.

It is the western wing of the fourth floor of a great university hospital. An abortion is about to take place. I am present because I asked to be present. I wanted to see what I had never seen.

The patient is Jamaican. She lies on the table submissively, and now and then she smiles at one of the nurses as though acknowledging a secret.

A nurse draws down the sheet, lays bare the abdomen. The belly mounds gently in the twenty-fourth week of pregnancy. The chief surgeon paints it with a sponge soaked in red antiseptic. He does this three times, each time a fresh sponge. He covers the area with a sterile sheet, an aperture in its center. He is a kindly man who teaches as he works, who pauses to reassure the woman.

He begins.

A little pinprick, he says to the woman.

He inserts the point of a tiny needle at the midline of the lower portion of her abdomen, on the downslope. He infiltrates local anesthetic into the skin, where it forms a small white bubble.

The woman grimaces.

That is all you will feel, the doctor says. Except for a little pressure. But no more pain.

She smiles again. She seems to relax. She settles comfortably on the table. The worst is over.

The doctor selects a three-and-one-half-inch needle bearing a central stylet. He places the point at the site of the previous injection. He aims it straight up and down, perpendicular. Next he takes hold of her abdomen with his left hand, palming the womb, steadying it. He thrusts with his right hand. The needle sinks into the abdominal wall.

Oh, says the woman quietly.

But I guess it is not pain that she feels. It is more a recognition that the deed is being done.

Another thrust and he has speared the uterus.

We are in, he says.

He has felt the muscular wall of the organ gripping the shaft of his needle. A further slight pressure on the needle advances it a bit more. He takes his left hand from the woman's abdomen. He retracts the filament of the stylet from the barrel of the needle. A small geyser of pale yellow fluid erupts.

We are in the right place, says the doctor. Are you feeling any pain? he asks.

She smiles, shakes her head. She gazes at the ceiling.

In the room we are six: two physicians, two nurses, the patient, and me. The participants are busy, very attentive. I am not at all busy—but I am no less attentive. I want to see.

I see something! It is unexpected, utterly unexpected, like a disturbance in the earth, a tumultuous jarring. I see a movement—a small one. But I have seen it.

And then I see it again. And now I see that it is the hub of the needle in the woman's belly that has jerked. First to one side. Then to the other side. Once more it wobbles, is *tugged,* like a fishing line nibbled by a sunfish.

Again! And I *know!*

It is the *fetus* that worries thus. It is the fetus struggling against the needle. Struggling? How can that be? I think: *that cannot be.* I think: the fetus feels no pain, cannot feel fear, has no *motivation.* It is merely reflex.

I point to the needle.

It is a reflex, says the doctor.

By the end of the fifth month, the fetus weighs about one pound, is about twelve inches long. Hair is on the head. There are eyebrows, eyelashes. Pale pink nipples show on the chest. Nails are present, at the fingertips, at the toes.

At the beginning of the sixth month, the fetus can cry, can suck, can make a fist. He kicks, he punches. The mother can feel this, can *see* this. His eyelids, until now closed, can open. He may look up, down, sideways. His grip is very strong. He could support his weight by holding with one hand.

A reflex, the doctor says.

I hear him. But I saw something in that mass of cells *understand* that it must bob and butt. And I see it again! I have an impulse to shove to the table—it is just a step—seize that needle, pull it out.

We are not six, I think. We are *seven.*

Something strangles *there.* An effort, its effort, binds me to it.

I do not shove to the table. I take no little step. It would be . . . well, madness. Everyone here wants the needle where it is. Six do. No, *five* do.

I close my eyes. I see inside of the uterus. It is bathed in ruby gloom. I see the creature curled upon itself. Its knees are flexed. Its head is bent upon its chest. It is in fluid and gently rocks to the rhythm of the distant heartbeat.

It resembles . . . a sleeping infant.

Its place is entered by something. It is sudden. A point coming. A needle!

A spike of *daylight* pierces the chamber. Now the light is extinguished. The needle comes closer in the pool. The point grazes the thigh, and I stir. Perhaps I wake from dozing. The light is there again. I twist and straighten. My arms and legs *push.* My hand finds the shaft—grabs! I *grab.* I bend the needle this way and that. The point probes, touches on my belly. My mouth opens. Could I cry out? All is a commotion and a churning. There is a presence in the pool. An activity! The pool colors, reddens, darkens.

I open my eyes to see the doctor feeding a small plastic tube through the barrel of the needle into the uterus. Drops of pink fluid overrun the rim and spill onto the sheet. He withdraws the needle from around the plastic tubing. Now only the little tube protrudes from the woman's body. A nurse hands the physician a syringe loaded with a colorless liquid. He attaches it to the end of the tubing and injects it.

Prostaglandin, he says.

Ah well, prostaglandin—a substance found normally in the body. When given in concentrated dosage, it throws the uterus into vigorous contraction. In eight to twelve hours, the woman will expel the fetus.

The doctor detaches the syringe but does not remove the tubing.

In case we must do it over, he says.

He takes away the sheet. He places gauze pads over the tubing. Over all this he applies adhesive tape.

I know. We cannot feed the great numbers. There is no more room. I know, I know. It is a woman's right to refuse the risk, to decline the pain of childbirth. And an unwanted child is a very great burden. An unwanted .child is a burden to himself. I know.

And yet . . . there is the flick of that needle. I *saw* it. I saw . . . I *felt*—in that room, a pace away, life prodded, life fending off. I saw life avulsed*—swept by flood, blackening—then *out.*

---

*torn away—Eds.

There, says the doctor. It's all over. It wasn't too bad, was it? he says to the woman.

She smiles. It is all over. Oh, yes.

And who would care to imagine that from a moist and dark commencement six months before there would ripen the cluster and globule, the sprout and pouch of man?

And who would care to imagine that trapped within the laked pearl and a dowry of yoke would lie the earliest stuff of dream and memory?

It is a persona carried here as well as a person, I think. I think it is a signed piece, engraved with a hieroglyph of human genes.

I did not think this until I saw. The flick. The fending off.

Later, in the corridor, the doctor explains that the law does not permit abortion beyond the twenty-fourth week. That is when the fetus may be viable, he says. We stand together for a moment, and he tells of an abortion in which the fetus *cried* after it was passed.

What did you do? I ask him.

There was nothing *to* do but let it live, he says. It did very well, he says. A case of mistaken dates.

A Defense of Abortion

Judith Jarvis Thomson

Most opposition to abortion relies on the premise that the fetus is a human being, a person, from the moment of conception. The premise is argued for, but, as I think, not well. Take, for example, the most common argument. We are asked to notice that the development of a human being from conception through birth into childhood is continuous; then it is said that to draw a line, to choose a point in this development and say "before this point the thing is not a person, after this point it is a person" is to make an arbitrary choice, a choice for which in the nature of things no good reason can be given. It is concluded that the fetus is, or anyway that we had better say it is, a person from the moment of conception. But this conclusion does not follow. Similar things might be said about the development of an acorn into an oak tree, and it does not follow that acorns are oak trees, or that we had better say they are. Arguments of this form are sometimes called "slippery slope arguments"—the phrase is perhaps self-explanatory—and it is dismaying that opponents of abortion rely on them so heavily and uncritically.

I am inclined to agree, however, that the prospects for "drawing a line" in the development of the fetus look dim. I am inclined to think also that we shall probably have to agree that the fetus has already become a human person well before birth. Indeed, it comes as a surprise when one first learns how early in its life it begins to acquire human characteristics. By the tenth week, for example, it already has a face, arms and legs, fingers and toes; it has internal organs, and brain activity is detectable.[1] On the other hand, I think that the premise is false, that the fetus is not a person from the

From *Philosophy and Public Affairs* (Fall 1971): 47-66. Copyright © 1971 Princeton University Press. Reprinted by permission of Princeton University Press.

moment of conception. A newly fertilized ovum, a newly implanted clump of cells, is no more a person than an acorn is an oak tree. But I shall not discuss any of this. For it seems to me to be of great interest to ask what happens if, for the sake of argument, we allow the premise. How, precisely, are we supposed to get from there to the conclusion that abortion is morally impermissible? Opponents of abortion commonly spend most of their time establishing that the fetus is a person, and hardly any time explaining the step from there to the impermissibility of abortion. Perhaps they think the step too simple and obvious to require much comment. Or perhaps instead they are simply being economical in argument. Many of those who defend abortion rely on the premise that the fetus is not a person, but only a bit of tissue that will become a person at birth; and why pay out more arguments than you have to? Whatever the explanation, I suggest that the step they take is neither easy nor obvious, that it calls for closer examination than it is commonly given, and that when we do give it this closer examination we shall feel inclined to reject it.

I propose, then, that we grant that the fetus is a person from the moment of conception. How does the argument go from here? Something like this, I take it. Every person has a right to life. So the fetus has a right to life. No doubt the mother has a right to decide what shall happen in and to her body; everyone would grant that. But surely a person's right to life is stronger and more stringent than the mother's right to decide what happens in and to her body, and so outweighs it. So the fetus may not be killed; an abortion may not be performed.

It sounds plausible. But now let me ask you to imagine this. You wake up in the morning and find yourself back to back in bed with an unconscious violinist. A famous unconscious violinist. He has been found to have a fatal kidney ailment, and the Society of Music Lovers has canvassed all the available medical records and found that you alone have the right blood type to help. They have therefore kidnapped you, and last night the violinist's circulatory system was plugged into yours, so that your kidneys can be used to extract poisons from his blood as well as your own. The director of the hospital now tells you, "Look, we're sorry the Society of Music Lovers did this to you—we would never have permitted it if we had known. But still, they did it, and the violinist now is plugged into you. To unplug you would be to kill him. But never mind, it's only for nine months. By then he will have recovered from his ailment, and can safely be unplugged from you." Is it morally incumbent on you to accede to this situation? No doubt it would be very nice of you if you did, a great kindness. But do you *have* to accede to it? What if it were not nine months, but nine years? Or longer still? What if the director of the hospital says, "Tough luck, I agree, but you've now got to stay in bed, with the violinist plugged into you, for the rest of your life. Because remember this. All persons have a right to life, and violinists are persons. Granted you have a right to decide what happens in and to your body, but a person's right to life outweighs your right to decide what happens in and to your body. So you cannot ever be unplugged from him." I imagine you would regard this as outrageous, which suggests that something really is wrong with that plausible-sounding argument I mentioned a moment ago.

In this case, of course, you were kidnapped; you didn't volunteer for the operation that plugged the violinist into your kidneys. Can those who oppose abortion on the ground I mentioned make an exception for a pregnancy due to rape? Certainly. They can say that persons have a right to life only if they didn't come into existence because of rape; or they can say that all persons have a right to life, but that some have less of a right to life than others, in particular, that those who came into existence because of rape have less. But these statements have a rather unpleasant sound. Surely the question of whether you have a right to life at all, or how much of it you have, shouldn't turn on the question of whether or not you are the product of a rape. And in fact the people who oppose abortion on the ground I mentioned do not make this distinction, and hence do not make an exception in case of rape.

Nor do they make an exception for a case in which the mother has to spend the nine months of her pregnancy in bed. They would agree that would be a great pity, and hard on the mother; but all the same, all persons have a right to life, the fetus is a person, and so on. I suspect, in fact, that they would not make an exception for a case in which, miraculously enough, the pregnancy went on for nine years, or even the rest of the mother's life.

Some won't even make an exception for a case in which continuation of the pregnancy is likely to shorten the mother's life; they regard abortion as impermissible even to save the mother's life. Such cases are nowadays very rare, and many opponents of abortion do not accept this extreme view. All the same, it is a good place to begin: a number of points of interest come out in respect to it.

1. Let us call the view that abortion is impermissible even to save the mother's life "the extreme view." I want to suggest first that it does not issue from the argument I mentioned earlier without the addition of some fairly powerful premises. Suppose a woman has become pregnant, and now learns that she has a cardiac condition such that she will die if she carries the baby to term. What may be done for her? The fetus, being a person, has a right to life, but as the mother is a person too, so has she a right to life. Presumably they have an equal right to life. How is it supposed to come out that an abortion may not be performed? If mother and child have an equal right to life, shouldn't we perhaps flip a coin? Or should we add to the mother's right to life her right to decide what happens in and to her body, which everybody seems to be ready to grant—the sum

of her rights now outweighing the fetus's right to life?

The most familiar argument here is the following: We are told that performing the abortion would be directly killing[2] the child, whereas doing nothing would not be killing the mother, but only letting her die. Moreover, in killing the child, one would be killing an innocent person, for the child has committed no crime, and is not aiming at his mother's death. And then there are a variety of ways in which this might be continued. (1) But as directly killing an innocent person is always and absolutely impermissible, an abortion may not be performed. Or, (2) as directly killing an innocent person is murder, and murder is always and absolutely impermissible, an abortion may not be performed. Or, (3) as one's duty to refrain from directly killing an innocent person is more stringent than one's duty to keep a person from dying, an abortion may not be performed. Or, (4) if one's only options are directly killing an innocent person or letting a person die, one must prefer letting the person die, and thus an abortion may not be performed.[3]

Some people seem to have thought that these are not further premises which must be added if the conclusion is to be reached, but that they follow from the very fact that an innocent person has a right to life. But this seems to me to be a mistake, and perhaps the simplest way to show this is to bring out that while we must certainly grant that innocent persons have a right to life, the theses in (1) through (4) are all false. Take (2), for example. If directly killing an innocent person is murder, and thus impermissible, then the mother's directly killing the innocent person inside her is murder, and thus is impermissible. But it cannot seriously be thought to be murder if the mother performs an abortion on herself to save her life. It cannot seriously be said that she *must* refrain, that she *must* sit passively by and wait for her death. Let us look again at the case of you and the violinist. There you are, in bed with the violinist, and the director of the hospital says to you, "It's all most distressing, and I deeply sympathize, but you see this is putting an additional strain on your kidneys, and you'll be dead within the month. But you *have* to stay where you are all the same. Because unplugging you would be directly killing an innocent violinist, and that's murder, and that's impermissible." If anything in the world is true, it is that you do not commit murder, you do not do what is impermissible, if you reach around to your back and unplug yourself from that violinist to save your life.

The main focus of attention in writings on abortion has been on what a third party may or may not do in answer to a request from a woman for an abortion. This is in a way understandable. Things being as they are, there isn't much a woman can safely do to abort herself. So the question asked is what a third party may do, and what the mother may do, if it is mentioned at all, is deduced, almost as an after-thought, from what it is concluded that third parties may do. But it seems to me that to treat the matter in this way is to refuse to grant to the mother that very status of person which is so firmly insisted on for the fetus. For we cannot simply read off what a person may do from what a third party may do. Suppose you find youself trapped in a tiny house with a growing child. I mean a very tiny house, and a rapidly growing child—you are already up against the wall of the house and in a few minutes you'll be crushed to death. The child on the other hand won't be crushed to death; if nothing is done to stop him from growing he'll be hurt, but in the end he'll simply burst open the house and walk out a free man. Now I could well understand it if a bystander were to say. "There's nothing we can do for you. We cannot choose between your life and his, we cannot be the ones to decide who is to live, we cannot intervene." But it cannot be concluded that you too can do nothing, that you cannot attack it to save your life. However innocent the child may be, you do not have to wait passively while it crushes you to death. Perhaps a pregnant woman is vaguely felt to have the status of house, to which we don't allow the right of self-defense. But if the woman houses the child, it should be remembered that she is a person who houses it.

I should perhaps stop to say explicitly that I am not claiming that people have a right to do anything whatever to save their lives. I think, rather, that there are drastic limits to the right of self-defense. If someone threatens you with death unless you torture someone else to death, I think you have not the right, even to save your life, to do so. But the case under consideration here is very different. In our case there are only two people involved, one whose life is threatened, and one who threatens it. Both are innocent: the one who is threatened is not threatened because of any fault, the one who threatens does not threaten because of any fault. For this reason we may feel that we bystanders cannot intervene. But the person threatened can.

In sum, a woman surely can defend her life against the threat to it posed by the unborn child, even if doing so involves its death. And this shows not merely that the theses in (1) through (4) are false; it shows also that the extreme view of abortion is false, and so we need not canvass any other possible ways of arriving at it from the argument I mentioned at the outset.

2. The extreme view could of course be weakened to say that while abortion is permissible to save the mother's life, it may not be performed by a third party, but only by the mother herself. But this cannot be right either. For what we have to keep in mind is that the mother and the unborn child are not like two tenants in a small house which has, by an unfortunate mistake, been rented to both: the mother *owns* the house. The fact that she does adds to the offensiveness of deducing that the mother can do nothing from the supposition that third parties can do nothing. But it does more than this: it casts a bright light on the supposition that third parties can

do nothing. Certainly it lets us see that a third party who says "I cannot choose between you" is fooling himself if he thinks this is impartiality. If Jones has found and fastened on a certain coat, which he needs to keep him from freezing, but which Smith also needs to keep him from freezing, then it is not impartiality that says "I cannot choose between you" when Smith owns the coat. Women have said again and again "This body is *my* body!" and they have reason to feel angry, reason to feel that it has been like shouting into the wind. Smith, after all, is hardly likely to bless us if we say to him, "Of course it's your coat, anybody would grant that it is. But no one may choose between you and Jones who is to have it."

We should really ask what it is that says "no one may choose" in the face of the fact that the body that houses the child is the mother's body. It may be simply a failure to appreciate this fact. But it may be something more interesting, namely the sense that one has a right to refuse to lay hands on people, even where it would be just and fair to do so, even where justice seems to require that somebody do so. Thus justice might call for somebody to get Smith's coat back from Jones, and yet you have a right to refuse to be the one to lay hands on Jones, a right to refuse to do physical violence to him. This, I think, must be granted. But then what should be said is not "no one may choose," but only "*I* cannot choose," and indeed not even this, but "*I* will not *act*," leaving it open that somebody else can or should, and in particular that anyone in a position of authority, with the job of securing people's rights, both can and should. So this is no difficulty. I have not been arguing that any given third party must accede to the mother's request that he perform an abortion to save her life, but only that he may.

I suppose that in some views of human life the mother's body is only on loan to her, the loan not being one which gives her any prior claim to it. One who held this view might well think it impartiality to say "I cannot choose." But I shall simply ignore this possibility. My own view is that if a human being has any just, prior claim to anything at all, he has a just, prior claim to his own body. And perhaps this needn't be argued for here anyway, since, as I mentioned, the arguments against abortion we are looking at do grant that the woman has a right to decide what happens in and to her body.

But although they do grant it, I have tried to show that they do not take seriously what is done in granting it. I suggest the same thing will reappear even more clearly when we turn away from cases in which the mother's life is at stake, and attend, as I propose we now do, to the vastly more common cases in which a woman wants an abortion for some less weighty reason than preserving her own life.

3. Where the mother's life is not at stake, the argument I mentioned at the outset seems to have a much stronger pull. "Everyone has a right

to life, so the unborn person has a right to life." And isn't the child's right to life weightier than anything other than the mother's own right to life, which she might put forward as ground for an abortion?

This argument treats the right to life as if it were unproblematic. It is not, and this seems to me to be precisely the source of the mistake.

For we should now, at long last, ask what it comes to, to have a right to life. In some views having a right to life includes having a right to be given at least the bare minimum one needs for continued life. But suppose that what in fact *is* the bare minimum a man needs for continued life is something he has no right at all to be given? If I am sick unto death, and the only thing that will save my life is the touch of [Robert Redford's]* cool hand on my fevered brow, then all the same, I have no right to be given the touch of [Robert Redford's] cool hand on my fevered brow. It would be frightfully nice of him to fly in from the West Coast to provide it. It would be less nice, though no doubt well meant, if my friends flew out to the West Coast and carried [Robert Redford] back with them. But I have no right at all against anybody that he should do this for me. Or again, to return to the story I told earlier, the fact that for continued life that violinist needs the continued use of your kidneys does not establish that he has a right to be given the continued use of your kidneys. He certainly has no right against you that *you* should give him continued use of your kidneys. For nobody has any right to use your kidneys unless you give him such a right; and nobody has the right against you that you shall give him this right—if you do allow him to go on using your kidneys, this is a kindness on your part, and not something he can claim from you as his due. Nor has he any right against anybody else that *they* should give him continued use of your kidneys. Certainly he had no right against the Society of Music Lovers that they should plug him into you in the first place. And if you now start to unplug yourself, having learned that you will otherwise have to spend nine years in bed with him, there is nobody in the world who must try to prevent you, in order to see to it that he is given something he has a right to be given.

Some people are rather stricter about the right to life. In their view, it does not include the right to be given anything, but amounts to, and only to, the right not to be killed by anybody. But here a related difficulty arises. If everybody is to refrain from killing that violinist, then everybody must refrain from doing a great many different sorts of things. Everybody must refrain from slitting his throat, everybody must refrain from shooting him—and everybody must refrain from unplugging you from him. But does he have a right against everybody that they shall refrain from unplugging

---

*At the time Dr. Thomson wrote this essay, she used the name of actor Henry Fonda to assist in making her point here. Mr. Fonda has since died, so to maintain the thrust of Dr. Thomson's point, we have substituted the name of a prominent male actor.—Eds.

you from him? To refrain from doing this is to allow him to continue to use your kidneys. It could be argued that he has a right against us that *we* should allow him to continue to use your kidneys. That is, while he had no right against us that we should give him the use of your kidneys, it might be argued that he anyway has a right against us that we shall not now intervene and deprive him of the use of your kidneys. I shall come back to third-party interventions later. But certainly the violinist has no right against you that *you* shall allow him to continue to use your kidneys. As I said, if you do allow him to use them, it is a kindness on your part, and not something you owe him.

The difficulty I point to here is not peculiar to the right to life. It reappears in connection with all the other natural rights; and it is something which an adequate account of rights must deal with. For present purposes it is enough just to draw attention to it. But I would stress that I am not arguing that people do not have a right to life—quite to the contrary, it seems to me that the primary control we must place on the acceptability of an account of rights is that it should turn out in that account to be a truth that all persons have a right to life. I am arguing only that having a right to life does not guarantee having either a right to be given the use of or a right to be allowed continued use of another person's body—even if one needs it for life itself. So the right to life will not serve the opponents of abortion in the very simple and clear way in which they seem to have thought it would.

4. There is another way to bring out the difficulty. In the most ordinary sort of case, to deprive someone of what he has a right to is to treat him unjustly. Suppose a boy and his small brother are jointly given a box of chocolates for Christmas. If the older boy takes the box and refuses to give his brother any of the chocolates, he is unjust to him, for the brother has been given a right to half of them. But suppose that, having learned that otherwise it means nine years in bed with that violinist, you unplug yourself from him. You surely are not being unjust to him, for you gave him no right to use your kidneys, and no one else can have given him any such right. But we have to notice that in unplugging yourself, you are killing him; and violinists, like everybody else, have a right to life, and thus in the view we were considering just now, the right not to be killed. So here you do what he supposedly has a right you shall not do, but you do not act unjustly to him in doing it.

The emendation which may be made at this point is this: the right to life consists not in the right not to be killed, but rather in the right not to be killed unjustly. This runs a risk of circularity, but never mind: it would enable us to square the fact that the violinist has a right to life with the fact that you do not act unjustly toward him in unplugging yourself, thereby killing him. For if you do not kill him unjustly, you do not violate his right to life, and so it is no wonder you do him no injustice.

But if this emendation is accepted, the gap in the argument against abortion stares us plainly in the face: it is by no means enough to show that the fetus is a person, and to remind us that all persons have a right to life—we need to be shown also that killing the fetus violates its right to life, i.e., that abortion is unjust killing. And is it?

I suppose we may take it as a datum that in a case of pregnancy due to rape the mother has not given the unborn person a right to the use of her body for food and shelter. Indeed, in what pregnancy could it be supposed that the mother has given the unborn person such a right? It is not as if there were unborn persons drifting about the world, to whom a woman who wants a child says "I invite you in."

But it might be argued that there are other ways one can have acquired a right to the use of another person's body than by having been invited to use it by that person. Suppose a woman voluntarily indulges in intercourse, knowing of the chance it will issue in pregnancy, and then she does become pregnant; is she not in part responsible for the presence, in fact the very existence, of the unborn person inside her? No doubt she did not invite it in. But doesn't her partial responsibility for its being there itself give it a right to the use of her body? If so, then her aborting it would be more like the boy's taking away the chocolates, and less like your unplugging yourself from the violinist—doing so would be depriving it of what it does have a right to, and thus would be doing it an injustice.

And then, too, it might be asked whether or not she can kill it even to save her own life: If she voluntarily called it into existence, how can she now kill it, even in self-defense?

The first thing to be said about this is that it is something new. Opponents of abortion have been so concerned to make out the independence of the fetus, in order to establish that it has a right to life, just as its mother does, that they have tended to overlook the possible support they might gain from making out that the fetus is *dependent* on the mother, in order to establish that she has a special kind of responsibility for it, a responsibility that gives it rights against her which are not possessed by any independent person—such as an ailing violinist who is a stranger to her.

On the other hand, this argument would give the unborn person a right to its mother's body only if her pregnancy resulted from a voluntary act, undertaken in full knowledge of the chance a pregnancy might result from it. It would leave out entirely the unborn person whose existence is due to rape. Pending the availability of some further argument, then, we would be left with the conclusion that unborn persons whose existence is due to rape have no right to the use of their mothers' bodies, and thus that aborting them is not depriving them of anything they have a right to and hence is not unjust killing.

And we should also notice that it is not at all plain that this argument really does go even as far as it purports to. For there are cases and cases, and the details make a difference. If the room is stuffy, and I therefore open a window to air it, and a burglar climbs in, it would be absurd to say, "Ah, now he can stay, she's given him a right to the use of her house—for she is partially responsible for his presence there, having voluntarily done what enabled him to get in, in full knowledge that there are such things as burglars, and that burglars burgle." It would be still more absurd to say this if I had had bars installed outside my windows, precisely to prevent burglars from getting in, and a burglar got in only because of a defect in the bars. It remains equally absurd if we imagine it is not a burglar who climbs in, but an innocent person who blunders or falls in. Again, suppose it were like this: people-seeds drift about in the air like pollen, and if you open your windows, one may drift in and take root in your carpets or upholstery. You don't want children, so you fix up your windows with fine mesh screens, the very best you can buy. As can happen, however, and on very, very rare occasions does happen, one of the screens is defective; and a seed drifts in and takes root. Does the person-plant who now develops have a right to the use of your house? Surely not—despite the fact that you voluntarily opened your windows, you knowingly kept carpets and upholstered furniture, and you knew that screens were sometimes defective. Someone may argue that you are responsible for its rooting, that it does have a right to your house, because after all you *could* have lived out your life with bare floors and furniture, or with sealed windows and doors. But this won't do—for by the same token anyone can avoid a pregnancy due to rape by having a hysterectomy, or anyway by never leaving home without a (reliable!) army.

It seems to me that the argument we are looking at can establish at most that there are *some* cases in which the unborn person has a right to the use of its mother's body, and therefore *some* cases in which abortion is unjust killing. There is room for much discussion and argument as to precisely which, if any. But I think we should sidestep this issue and leave it open, for at any rate the argument certainly does not establish that all abortion is unjust killing.

5. There is room for yet another argument here, however. We surely must all grant that there may be cases in which it would be morally indecent to detach a person from your body at the cost of his life. Suppose you learn that what the violinist needs is not nine years of your life, but only one hour: all you need to do to save his life is to spend one hour in that bed with him. Suppose also that letting him use your kidneys for that one hour would not affect your health in the slightest. Admittedly you were kidnapped. Admittedly you did not give anyone permission to plug him

into you. Nevertheless it seems to me plain you *ought* to allow him to use your kidneys for that hour—it would be indecent to refuse.

Again, suppose pregnancy lasted only an hour, and constituted no threat to life or health. And suppose that a woman becomes pregnant as a result of rape. Admittedly she did not voluntarily do anything to bring about the existence of a child. Admittedly she did nothing at all which would give the unborn person a right to the use of her body. All the same it might well be said, as in the newly emended violinist story, that she *ought* to allow it to remain for that hour—that it would be indecent in her to refuse.

Now some people are inclined to use the term "right" in such a way that it follows from the fact that you ought to allow a person to use your body for the hour he needs, that he has a right to use your body for the hour he needs, even though he has not been given that right by any person or act. They may say that it follows also that if you refuse, you act unjustly toward him. This use of the term is perhaps so common that it cannot be called wrong; nevertheless it seems to me to be an unfortunate loosening of what we would do better to keep a tight rein on. Suppose that box of chocolates I mentioned earlier had not been given to both boys jointly, but was given only to the older boy. There he sits, stolidly eating his way through the box, his small brother watching enviously. Here we are likely to say "You ought not to be so mean. You ought to give your brother some of those chocolates." My own view is that it just does not follow from the truth of this that the brother has any right to any of the chocolates. If the boy refuses to give his brother any, he is greedy, stingy, callous—but not unjust. I suppose that the people I have in mind will say it does follow that the brother has a right to some of the chocolates, and thus that the boy does act unjustly if he refuses to give his brother any. But the effect of saying this is to obscure what we should keep distinct, namely the difference between the boy's refusal in this case and the boy's refusal in the earlier case, in which the box was given to both boys jointly, and in which the small brother thus had what was from any point of view clear title to half.

A further objection to so using the term "right" that from the fact that A ought to do a thing for B, it follows that B has a right against A that A do it for him, is that it is going to make the question of whether or not a man has a right to a thing turn on how easy it is to provide him with it; and this seems not merely unfortunate, but morally unacceptable. Take the case of [Robert Redford] again. I said earlier that I had no right to the touch of his cool hand on my fevered brow, even though I needed it to save my life. I said it would be frightfully nice of him to fly in from the West Coast to provide me with it, but that I had no right against him that he should do so. But suppose he isn't on the West Coast. Suppose he has only to walk across the room, place a hand briefly on my brow—

and lo, my life is saved. Then surely he ought to do it, it would be indecent to refuse. Is it to be said "Ah, well, it follows that in this case she has a right to the touch of his hand on her brow, and so it would be an injustice in him to refuse"? So that I have a right to it when it is easy for him to provide it, though no right when it's hard? It's rather a shocking idea that anyone's rights should fade away and disappear as it gets harder and harder to accord them to him.

So my own view is that even though you ought to let the violinist use your kidneys for the one hour he needs, we should not conclude that he has a right to do so—we should say that if you refuse, you are, like the boy who owns all the chocolates and will give none away, self-centered and callous, indecent in fact, but not unjust. And similarly, that even supposing a case in which a woman pregnant due to rape ought to allow the unborn person to use her body for the hour he needs, we should not conclude that he has a right to do so; we should conclude that she is self-centered, callous, indecent, but not unjust, if she refuses. The complaints are no less grave; they are just different. However, there is no need to insist on this point. If anyone does wish to deduce "he has a right" from "you ought," then all the same he must surely grant that there are cases in which it is not morally required of you that you allow that violinist to use your kidneys, and in which he does not have a right to use them, and in which you do not do him an injustice if you refuse. And so also for mother and unborn child. Except in such cases as the unborn person has a right to demand it—and we were leaving open the possibility that there may be such cases—nobody is morally *required* to make large sacrifices, of health, of all other interests and concerns, of all other duties and commitments, for nine years, or even for nine months, in order to keep another person alive.

6. We have in fact to distinguish between two kinds of Samaritan: the Good Samaritan and what we might call the Minimally Decent Samaritan. The story of the Good Samaritan, you will remember, goes like this:

A certain man went down from Jerusalem to Jericho, and fell among thieves, which stripped him of his raiment, and wounded him, and departed, leaving him half dead.

And by chance there came down a certain priest that way; and when he saw him, he passed by on the other side.

And likewise a Levite, when he was at the place, came and looked on him, and passed by on the other side.

But a certain Samaritan, as he journeyed, came where he was; and when he saw him he had compassion on him.

And went to him, and bound up his wounds, pouring in oil and wine, and set him on his own beast, and brought him to an inn, and took care of him.

And on the morrow, when he departed, he took out two pence, and
gave them to the host, and said unto him, "Take care of him; and whatsoever
thou spendest more, when I come again, I will repay thee." (Luke 10:30-
35)

The Good Samaritan went out of his way, at some cost to himself, to help
one in need of it. We are not told what the options were, that is, whether
or not the priest and the Levite could have helped by doing less than the
Good Samaritan did, but assuming they could have, then the fact they did
nothing at all shows they were not even Minimally Decent Samaritans, not
because they were not Samaritans, but because they were not even minimally decent.

These things are a matter of degree, of course, but there is a difference,
and it comes out perhaps most clearly in the story of Kitty Genovese, who,
as you will remember, was murdered while thirty-eight people watched or
listened, and did nothing at all to help her. A Good Samaritan would have
rushed out to give direct assistance against the murderer. Or perhaps we
had better allow that it would have been a Splendid Samaritan who did
this, on the ground that it would have involved a risk of death for himself.
But the thirty-eight not only did not do this, they did not even trouble
to pick up a phone to call the police. Minimally Decent Samaritanism would
call for doing at least that, and their not having done it was monstrous.

After telling the story of the Good Samaritan, Jesus said "Go, and
do thou likewise." Perhaps he meant that we are morally required to act
as the Good Samaritan did. Perhaps he was urging people to do more
than is morally required of them. At all events it seems plain that it was
not morally required of any of the thirty-eight that he rush out to give
direct assistance at the risk of his own life, and that it is not morally required of anyone that he give long stretches of his life—nine years or nine
months—to sustaining the life of a person who has no special right (we
were leaving open the possibility of this) to demand it.

Indeed, with one rather striking class of exceptions, no one in any country in the world is *legally* required to do anywhere near as much as this
for anyone else. The class of exceptions is obvious. My main concern here
is not the state of the law in respect to abortion, but it is worth drawing
attention to the fact that in no state in this country is any man compelled
by law to be even a Minimally Decent Samaritan to any person; there
is no law under which charges could be brought against the thirty-eight
who stood by while Kitty Genovese died. By contrast, in most states in
this country women are compelled by law to be not merely Minimally Decent Samaritans, but Good Samaritans to unborn persons inside them.*

---

*The reader is reminded that this article was published before the U.S. Supreme Court
rendered its decison in *Roe* v. *Wade.*—Eds.

This doesn't by itself settle anything one way or the other, because it may well be argued that there should be laws in this country—as there are in many European countries—compelling at least Minimally Decent Samaritanism. But it does show that there is a gross injustice in the existing state of the law. And it shows also that the groups currently working against liberalization of abortion laws, in fact working toward having it declared unconstitutional for a state to permit abortion, had better start working for the adoption of Good Samaritan laws generally, or earn the charge that they are acting in bad faith.

I should think, myself, that Minimally Decent Samaritan laws would be one thing, Good Samaritan laws quite another, and in fact highly improper. But we are not here concerned with the law. What we should ask is not whether anybody should be compelled by law to be a Good Samaritan, but whether we must accede to a situation in which somebody is being compelled—by nature, perhaps—to be a Good Samaritan. We have, in other words, to look now at third-party interventions. I have been arguing that no person is morally required to make large sacrifices to sustain the life of another who has no right to demand them, and this even where the sacrifices do not include life itself; we are not morally required to be Good Samaritans or anyway Very Good Samaritans to one another. But what if a man cannot extricate himself from such a situation? What if he appeals to us to extricate him? It seems to me plain that there are cases in which we can, cases in which a Good Samaritan would extricate him. There you are, you were kidnapped, and nine years in bed with that violinist lie ahead of you. You have your own life to lead. You are sorry, but you simply cannot see giving up so much of your life to the sustaining of his. You cannot extricate yourself, and ask us to do so. I should have thought that—in light of his having no right to the use of your body— it was obvious that we do not have to accede to your being forced to give up so much. We can do what you ask. There is no injustice to the violinist in our doing so.

7. Following the lead of the opponents of abortion. I have throughout been speaking of the fetus merely as a person, and what I have been asking is whether or not the argument we began with, which proceeds only from the fetus's being a person, really does establish its conclusion. I have argued that it does not.

But of course there are arguments and arguments, and it may be said that I have simply fastened on the wrong one. It may be said that what is important is not merely the fact that the fetus is a person, but that it is a person for whom the woman has a special kind of responsibility issuing from the fact that she is its mother. And it might be argued that all my analogies are therefore irrelevant—for you do not have that special kind of responsibility for that violinist, [Robert Redford] does not have that special kind of responsibility for me. And our attention might be drawn to the fact that men and women both *are* compelled by law to provide support for their children.

I have in effect dealt (briefly) with this argument in section 4 above; but a (still briefer) recapitulation now may be in order. Surely we do not have any such "special responsibility" for a person unless we have assumed it, explicitly or implicitly. If a set of parents do not try to prevent pregnancy, do not obtain an abortion, and then at the time of birth of the child do not put it out for adoption, but rather take it home with them, then they have assumed responsibility for it, they have given it rights, and they cannot *now* withdraw support from it at the cost of its life because they now find it difficult to go on providing for it. But if they have taken all reasonable precautions against having a child, they do not simply by virtue of their biological relationship to the child who comes into existence have a special responsibility for it. They may wish to assume responsibility for it, or they may not wish to. And I am suggesting that if assuming responsibility for it would require large sacrifices, then they may refuse. A Good Samaritan would not refuse—or anyway, a Splendid Samaritan, if the sacrifices that had to be made were enormous. But then so would a Good Samaritan assume responsibility for that violinist; so would [Robert Redford], if he is a Good Samaritan, fly in from the West Coast and assume responsibility for me.

8. My argument will be found unsatisfactory on two counts by many of those who want to regard abortion as morally permissible. First, while I do argue that abortion is not impermissible, I do not argue that it is always permissible. There may well be cases in which carrying the child to term requires only Minimally Decent Samaritanism of the mother, and this is a standard we must not fall below. I am inclined to think it a merit of my account precisely that it does *not* give a general yes or a general no. It allows for and supports our sense that, for example, a sick and desperately frightened fourteen-year-old schoolgirl, pregnant due to rape, may *of course* choose abortion, and that any law which rules this out is an insane law. And it also allows for and supports our sense that in other cases resort to abortion is even positively indecent. It would be indecent in the woman to request an abortion, and indecent in a doctor to perform it, if she is in her seventh month, and wants the abortion just to avoid the nuisance of postponing a trip abroad. The very fact that the arguments I have been drawing attention to treat all cases of abortion, or even all cases of abortion in which the mother's life is not at stake, as morally on a par ought to have made them suspect at the outset.

Secondly, while I am arguing for the permissibility of abortion in some cases, I am not arguing for the right to secure the death of the unborn child. It is easy to confuse these two things in that up to a certain point in the life of the fetus it is not able to survive outside the mother's body;

hence removing it from her body guarantees its death. But they are importantly different. I have argued that you are not morally required to spend nine months in bed, sustaining the life of that violinist; but to say this is by no means to say that if, when you unplug yourself, there is a miracle and he survives, you then have a right to turn around and slit his throat. You may detach yourself even if this costs him his life; you have no right to be guaranteed his death, by some other means, if unplugging yourself does not kill him. There are some people who will feel dissatisfied by this feature of my argument. A woman may be utterly devastated by the thought of a child, a bit of herself, put out for adoption and never seen or heard of again. She may therefore want not merely that the child be detached from her, but more, that it die. Some opponents of abortion are inclined to regard this as beneath contempt—thereby showing insensitivity to what is surely a powerful source of despair. All the same, I agree that the desire for the child's death is not one which anybody may gratify, should it turn out to be possible to detach the child alive.

At this place, however, it should be remembered that we have only been pretending throughout that the fetus is a human being from the moment of conception. A very early abortion is surely not the killing of a person, and so is not dealt with by anything I have said here.

NOTES

1. Daniel Callahan, *Abortion: Law, Choice and Morality* (New York, 1970), p. 373. This book gives a fascinating survey of the available information on abortion. The Jewish tradition is surveyed in David M. Feldman, *Birth Control in Jewish Law* (New York, 1968), Part 5, the Catholic tradition in John T. Noonan, Jr., "An Almost Absolute Value in History," in *The Morality of Abortion*, ed. John T. Noonan, Jr. (Cambridge, Mass., 1970).

2. The term "direct" in the arguments I refer to is a technical one. Roughly, what is meant by "direct killing" is either killing as an end in itself, or killing as a means to some end, for example, the end of saving someone else's life.

3. The thesis in (4) is in an interesting way weaker than those in (1), (2), and (3): they rule out abortion even in cases in which both mother *and* child will die if the abortion is not performed. By contrast, one who held the view expressed in (4) could consistently say that one needn't prefer letting two persons die to killing one.

Abortion and Infanticide

Michael Tooley

This essay deals with the question of the morality of abortion and infanticide. The fundamental ethical objection traditionally advanced against these practices rests on the contention that human fetuses and infants have a right to life. It is this claim which will be the focus of attention here. The basic issue to be discussed, then, is what properties a thing must possess in order to have a serious right to life. My approach will be to set out and defend a basic moral principle specifying a condition an organism must satisfy if it is to have a serious right to life. It will be seen that this condition is not satisfied by human fetuses and infants, and thus that they do not have a right to life. So unless there are other substantial objections to abortion and infanticide, one is forced to conclude that these practices are morally acceptable ones. In contrast, it may turn out that our treatment of adult members of other species—cats, dogs, polar bears—is morally indefensible. For it is quite possible that such animals do possess properties that endow them with a right to life.

I. ABORTION AND INFANTICIDE

One reason the question of the morality of infanticide is worth examining is that it seems very difficult to formulate a completely satisfactory liberal position on abortion without coming to grips with the infanticide issue. The problem the liberal encounters is essentially that of specifying a cutoff point which is not arbitrary: at what stage in the development of a human

From *Philosophy & Public Affairs* 2 (Fall 1972): pp. 37-65. Copyright © 1972 Princeton University Press. Reprinted with permission of Princeton University Press.

being does it cease to be morally permissible to destroy it? It is important to be clear about the difficulty here. The conservative's objection is not that since there is a continuous line of development from a zygote to a newborn baby, one must conclude that if it is seriously wrong to destroy a newborn baby it is also seriously wrong to destroy a zygote or any intermediate stage in the development of a human being. His point is rather that if one says it is wrong to destroy a newborn baby but not a zygote or some intermediate stage in the development of a human being, one should be prepared to point to a *morally relevant* difference between a newborn baby and the earlier stage in the development of a human being.

Precisely the same difficulty can, of course, be raised for a person who holds that infanticide is morally permissible. The conservative will ask what morally relevant differences there are between an adult human being and a newborn baby. What makes it morally permissible to destroy a baby, but wrong to kill an adult? So the challenge remains. But I will argue that in this case there is an extremely plausible answer.

Reflecting on the morality of infanticide forces one to face up to this challenge. In the case of abortion a number of events—quickening or viability, for instance—might be taken as cutoff points, and it is easy to overlook the fact that none of these events involves any morally significant change in the developing human. In contrast, if one is going to defend infanticide, one has to get very clear about what makes something a person, what gives something a right to life. . . .

Aside from the light it may shed on the abortion question, the issue of infanticide is both interesting and important in its own right. The theoretical interest has been mentioned: it forces one to face up to the question of what makes something a person. The practical importance need not be labored. Most people would prefer to raise children who do not suffer from gross deformities or from severe physical, emotional, or intellectual handicaps. If it could be shown that there is no moral objection to infanticide the happiness of society could be significantly and justifiably increased.

Infanticide is also of interest because of the strong emotions it arouses. The typical reaction to infanticide is like the reaction to incest or cannibalism, or the reaction of previous generations to masturbation or oral sex. The response, rather than appealing to carefully formulated moral principles, is primarily visceral. When philosophers themselves respond in this way, offering no arguments, and dismissing infanticide out of hand, it is reasonable to suspect that one is dealing with a taboo rather than with a rational prohibition.[1] I shall attempt to show that this is in fact the case.

II. TERMINOLOGY: "PERSON" VERSUS "HUMAN BEING"

How is the term "person" to be interpreted? I shall treat the concept of a person as a purely moral concept, free of all descriptive content. Specifically, in my usage the sentence "X is a person" will be synonymous with the sentence "X has a (serious) moral right to life."

* * *

The tendency to use expressions like "person" and "human being" interchangeably is an unfortunate one. For one thing, it tends to lend covert support to antiabortionist positions. Given such usage, one who holds a liberal view of abortion is put in the position of maintaining that fetuses, at least up to a certain point, are not human beings. . . . Thus Wertheimer says that "except for monstrosities, every member of our species is indubitably a person, a human being, at the very latest at birth.[2] Is it really *indubitable* that newborn babies are persons? . . . Wertheimer is falling prey to the confusion naturally engendered by the practice of using "person" and "human being" interchangeably. . . .

There is a second reason why using "person" and "human being" interchangeably is unhappy philosophically. If one says that the dispute between pro- and anti-abortionists centers on whether the fetus is a human, it is natural to conclude that it is essentially a disagreement about certain facts, a disagreement about what properties a fetus possesses. Thus Wertheimer says that "if one insists on using the raggy fact-value distinction, then one ought to say that the dispute is over a matter of fact in the sense in which it is a fact that the Negro slaves were human beings."[3] I shall argue that the two cases are not parallel, and that in the case of abortion what is primarily at stake is what moral principles one should accept. If one says that the central issue between conservatives and liberals in the abortion question is whether the fetus is a person, it is clear that the dispute may be either about what properties a thing must have in order to be a person, in order to have a right to life—a moral question—or about whether a fetus at a given stage of development as a matter of fact possesses the properties in question. The temptation to suppose that the disagreement must be a factual one is removed.

It should now be clear why the common practice of using expressions such as "person" and "'human being" interchangeably in discussions of abortion is unfortunate. . . . My own approach will be to use the term "human" only in contexts where it is not philosophically dangerous.

III. THE BASIC ISSUE: WHEN IS A MEMBER OF THE SPECIES *HOMO SAPIENS* A PERSON?

Settling the issue of the morality of abortion and infanticide will involve answering the following questions: What properties must something have to be a person, i.e., to have a serious right to life? At what point in the development of a member of the species *Homo sapiens* does the organism possess the properties that make it a person? The first question raises a moral issue. To answer it is to decide what basic[4] moral principles involving the ascription of a right to life one ought to accept. The second question raises a purely factual issue, since the properties in question are properties of a purely descriptive sort.

Some writers seem quite pessimistic about the possibility of resolving the question of the morality of abortion. Indeed, some have gone so far as to suggest that the question of whether the fetus is a person is in principle unanswerable: "we seem to be stuck with the indeterminateness of the fetus's humanity."[5] An understanding of some of the sources of this pessimism will, I think, help us to tackle the problem. Let us begin by considering the similarity a number of people have noted between the issue of abortion and the issue of Negro slavery. The question here is why it should be more difficult to decide whether abortion and infanticide are acceptable than it was to decide whether slavery was acceptable. The answer seems to be that in the case of slavery there are moral principles of a quite uncontroversial sort that settle the issue. Thus most people would agree to some such principle as the following: No organism that has experiences, that is capable of thought and of using language, and that has harmed no one, should be made a slave. In the case of abortion, on the other hand, conditions that are generally agreed to be sufficient grounds for ascribing a right to life to something do not suffice to settle the issue. It is easy to specify other, purportedly sufficient conditions that will settle the issue, but no one has been successful in putting forward considerations that will convince others to accept those additional moral principles.

I do not share the general pessimism about the possibility of resolving the issue of abortion and infanticide because I believe it is possible to point to a very plausible moral principle dealing with the question of *necessary* conditions for something's having a right to life, where the conditions in question will provide an answer to the question of the permissibility of abortion and infanticide.

There is a second cause of pessimism that should be noted before proceeding. It is tied up with the fact that the development of an organism is one of gradual and continuous change. Given this continuity, how is one to draw a line at one point and declare it permissible to destroy a member of *Homo sapiens* up to, but not beyond, that point? Won't there be an arbitrariness about any point that is chosen? I will return to this worry shortly. It does not present a serious difficulty once the basic moral principles relevant to the ascription of a right to life to an individual are established.

Let us turn now to the first and most fundamental question: What properties must something have in order to be a person, i.e., to have a serious right to life? The claim I wish to defend is this: An organism possesses a serious right to life only if it possesses the concept of a self as a continuing subject of experiences and other mental states, and believes that it is itself such a continuing entity.

My basic argument in support of this claim, which I will call the self-consciousness requirement, will be clearest, I think, if I first offer a simplified version of the argument, and then consider a modification that seems desirable. The simplified version of my argument is this. To ascribe a right to an individual is to assert something about the prima facie obligations of other individuals to act, or to refrain from acting, in certain ways. However, the obligations in question are conditional ones, being dependent upon the existence of certain desires of the individual to whom the right is ascribed. Thus if an individual asks one to destroy something to which he has a right, one does not violate his right to that thing if one proceeds to destroy it. This suggests the following analysis: "A has a right to X" is roughly synonymous with "If A desires X, then others are under a prima facie obligation to refrain from actions that would deprive him of it."[6]

Although this analysis is initially plausible, there are reasons for thinking it not entirely correct. I will consider these later. Even here, however, some expansion is necessary, since there are features of the concept of a right that are important in the present context, and that ought to be dealt with more explicitly. In particular, it seems to be a conceptual truth that things that lack consciousness, such as ordinary machines, cannot have rights. Does this conceptual truth follow from the above analysis of the concept of a right? The answer depends on how the term "desire" is interpreted. If one adopts a completely behavioristic interpretation of "desire," so that a machine that searches for an electrical outlet in order to get its batteries recharged is described as having a desire to be recharged, then it will follow from this analysis that objects that lack consciousness cannot have rights. On the other hand, if "desire" is interpreted in such a way that desires are states necessarily standing in some sort of relationship to states of consciousness, it will follow from the analysis that a machine that is not capable of being conscious, and consequently of having desires, cannot have any rights. I think those who defend analyses of the concept of a right along the lines of this one do have in mind an interpretation of the term "desire" that involves reference to something more than behavioral dispositions. However, rather than relying on this, it seems preferable to make such an interpretation explicit. The following analysis is a natural way of doing that: "A has a right to X" is roughly synonymous with "A is the sort of thing that is a subject of experiences and other mental states, A is capable of desiring X, and if A does desire X, then others are under a prima facie obligation to refrain from actions that would deprive him of it."

The next step in the argument is basically a matter of applying this analysis to the concept of a right to life. Unfortunately the expression "right to life" is not entirely a happy one, since it suggests that the right in question concerns the continued existence of a biological organism. That this is incorrect can be brought out by considering possible ways of violating an individual's right to life. Suppose, for example, that by some technology of the future the brain of an adult human were to be completely reprogrammed, so that the organism wound up with memories (or rather, apparent memories), beliefs, attitudes, and personality traits completely different from those associated with it before it was subjected to reprogramming. In such a case one would surely say that an individual had been destroyed, that an adult human's right to life had been violated, even though no biological organism had been killed. This example shows that the expression "right to life" is misleading, since what one is really concerned about is not just the continued existence of a biological organism, but the right of a subject of experiences and other mental states to continue to exist.

Given this more precise description of the right with which we are here concerned, we are now in a position to apply the analysis of the concept of a right stated above. When we do so we find that the statement "A has a right to continue to exist as a subject of experiences and other mental states" is roughly synonymous with the statement "A is a subject of experiences and other mental states, A is capable of desiring to continue to exist as a subject of experiences and other mental states, and if A does desire to continue to exist as such an entity, then others are under a prima facie obligation not to prevent him from doing so."

The final stage in the argument is simply a matter of asking what must be the case if something is to be capable of having a desire to continue existing as a subject of experiences and other mental states. The basic point here is that the desires a thing can have are limited by the concepts it possesses. For the fundamental way of describing a given desire is as a desire that a certain proposition be true.[7] Then, since one cannot desire that a certain proposition be true unless one understands it, and since one cannot understand it without possessing the concepts involved in it, it follows that the desires one can have are limited by the concepts one possesses. Applying this to the present case results in the conclusion that an entity cannot be the sort of thing that can desire that a subject of experiences and other mental states exist unless it possesses the concept of such a subject. Moreover, an entity cannot desire that it itself *continue* existing as a subject of experiences and other mental states unless it believes that it is now such a subject. This completes the justification of the claim that it is a necessary condition of something's having a serious right to life that it possess the concept of a self as a continuing subject of experiences, and that it believe that it is itself such an entity.

. . . Certain situations suggest that there may be exceptions to the claim that if a person doesn't desire something, one cannot violate his right to it. There are three types of situations that call this claim into question: (i) situations in which an individual's desires reflect a state of emotional disturbance; (ii) situations in which a previously conscious individual is temporarily unconscious; (iii) situations in which an individual's desires have been distorted by conditioning or by indoctrination.

As an example of the first, consider a case in which an adult human falls into a state of depression which his psychiatrist recognizes as temporary. While in the state he tells people he wishes he were dead. His psychiatrist, accepting the view that there can be no violation of an individual's right to life unless the individual has a desire to live, decides to let his patient have his way and kills him. . . .

The second set of situations are ones in which an individual is unconscious for some reason—that is, he is sleeping, or drugged, or in a temporary coma. Does an individual in such a state have any desires? . . .

Finally, consider situations in which an individual's desires have been distorted, either by inculcation of irrational beliefs or by direct conditioning. Thus an individual may permit someone to kill him because he has been convinced that if he allows himself to be sacrificed to the gods he will be gloriously rewarded in a life to come. . . .

Situations such as these strongly suggest that even if an individual doesn't want something, it is still possible to violate his right to it. Some modification of the earlier account of the concept of a right thus seems in order. The analysis given covers, I believe, the paradigmatic cases of violation of an individual's rights, but there are other, secondary cases where one also wants to say that someone's right has been violated. . . .

Here it will be sufficient merely to say that, in view of the above, an individual's right to X can be violated not only when he desires X, but also when he *would* now desire X were it not for one of the following: (i) he is in an emotionally unbalanced state; (ii) he is temporarily unconscious; (iii) he has been conditioned to desire the absence of X.

The critical point now is that, even given this extension of the conditions under which an individual's right to something can be violated, it is still true that one's right to something can be violated only when one has the conceptual capability of desiring the thing in question. For example, an individual who would now desire not to be a slave if he weren't emotionally unbalanced, or if he weren't temporarily unconscious, or if he hadn't previously been conditioned to want to be a slave, must possess the concepts involved in the desire not to be a slave. Since it is really only the conceptual capability presupposed by the desire to continue existing as a subject of experiences and other mental states, and not the desire itself, that enters into the above argument, the modification required in the account of the conditions under which an individual's rights can be violated does not undercut my defense of the self-consciousness requirement.

To sum up, my argument has been that having a right to life presupposes that one is capable of desiring to continue existing as a subject of experiences and other mental states. This in turn presupposes both that one has the concept of such a continuing entity and that one believes that one is oneself such an entity. So an entity that lacks such a consciousness of itself as a continuing subject of mental states does not have a right to life.

It would be natural to ask at this point whether satisfaction of this requirement is not only necessary but also sufficient to ensure that a thing has a right to life. I am inclined to an affirmative answer. However, the issue is not urgent in the present context, since as long as the requirement is in fact a necessary one we have the basis of an adequate defense of abortion and infanticide. If an organism must satisfy some other condition before it has a serious right to life, the result will merely be that the interval during which infanticide is morally permissible may be somewhat longer. Although the point at which an organism first achieves self-consciousness and hence the capacity of desiring to continue existing as a subject of experiences and other mental states may be a theoretically incorrect cutoff point, it is at least a morally safe one: any error it involves is on the side of caution.

IV. SOME CRITICAL COMMENTS ON ALTERNATIVE PROPOSALS

I now want to compare the line of demarcation I am proposing with the cutoff points traditionally advanced in discussions of abortion. My fundamental claim will be that none of these cutoff points can be defended by appeal to plausible, basic moral principles. The main suggestions as to the point past which it is seriously wrong to destroy something that will develop into an adult member of the species *Homo sapiens* are these: (a) conception; (b) the attainment of human form; (c) the achievement of the ability to move about spontaneously; (d) viability; (e) birth.[8] The corresponding moral principles suggested by these cutoff points are as follows: (1) It is seriously wrong to kill an organism, from a zygote on, that belongs to the species *Homo sapiens*. (2) It is seriously wrong to kill an organism that belongs to *Homo sapiens* and that has achieved human form. (3) It is seriously wrong to kill an organism that is a member of *Homo sapiens* and that is capable of spontaneous movement. (4) It is seriously wrong to kill an organism that belongs to *Homo sapiens* and that is capable of existing outside the womb. (5) It is seriously wrong to kill an organism that is a member of *Homo sapiens* that is no longer in the womb.

My first comment is that it would not do *simply* to omit the reference to membership in the species *Homo sapiens* from the above principles, with the exception of principle (2). For then the principle would be applicable to animals in general, and one would be forced to conclude that it was seriously wrong to abort a cat fetus, or that it was seriously wrong to abort a motile cat fetus, and so on.

The second and crucial comment is that none of the five principles given above can plausibly be viewed as a *basic* moral principle. To accept any of them as such would be akin to accepting as a basic moral principle the proposition that it is morally permissible to enslave black members of the species *Homo sapiens* but not white members. Why should it be seriously wrong to kill an unborn member of the species *Homo sapiens* but not seriously wrong to kill an unborn kitten? Difference in species is not per se a morally relevant difference. If one holds that it is seriously wrong to kill an unborn member of the species Homo sapiens but not an unborn kitten, one should be prepared to point to some property that is morally significant and that is possessed by unborn members of *Homo sapiens* but not by unborn kittens. Similarly, such a property must be identified if one believes it seriously wrong to kill unborn members of *Homo sapiens* that have achieved viability but not seriously wrong to kill unborn kittens that have achieved that state.

What property might account for such a difference? That is to say, what *basic* moral principles might a person who accepts one of these five principles appeal to in support of his secondary moral judgment? Why should events such as the achievement of human form, or the achievement of the ability to move about, or the achievement of viability, or birth serve to endow something with a right to life? What the liberal must do is to show that these events involve changes, or are associated with changes, that are morally relevant.

*   *   *

V. REFUTATION OF THE CONSERVATIVE POSITION

Many have felt that the conservative's position is more defensible than the liberal's because the conservative can point to the gradual and continuous development of an organism as it changes from a zygote to an adult human being. He is then in a position to argue that it is morally arbitrary for the liberal to draw a line at some point in this continuous process and to say that abortion is permissible before, but not after, that particular point. The liberal's reply would presumably be that the emphasis upon the continuity of the process is misleading. What the conservative is really doing is simply challenging the liberal to specify the properties a thing must have in order to be a person, and to show that the developing organism does acquire the properties at the point selected by the liberal. The liberal may then reply that the difficulty he has meeting this challenge should not be taken as grounds for rejecting his position. For the conservative cannot meet this challenge either; the conservative is equally unable to say what properties something must have if it is to have a right to life.

Although this rejoinder does not dispose of the conservative's argument, it is not without bite. For defenders of the view that abortion is always wrong have failed to face up to the question of the basic moral principles on which their position rests. They have been content to assert the wrongness of killing any organism, from a zygote on, if that organism is a member of the species *Homo sapiens*. But they have overlooked the point that this cannot be an acceptable *basic* moral principle, since difference in species is not in itself a morally relevant difference. The conservative can reply, however, that it is possible to defend his position—but not the liberal's— *without* getting clear about the properties a thing must possess if it is to have a right to life. The conservative's defense will rest upon the following two claims: first, that there is a property, even if one is unable to specify what it is, that (i) is possessed by adult humans, and (ii) endows any organism possessing it with a serious right to life. Second, that if there are properties which satisfy (i) and (ii) above, at least one of those properties will be such that any organism potentially possessing that property has a serious right to life even now, simply by virtue of that potentiality, where an organism possesses a property potentially if it will come to have that property in the normal course of its development. The second claim—which I shall refer to as the potentiality principle—is critical to the conservative's defense. Because of it he is able to defend his position without deciding what properties a thing must possess in order to have a right to life. It is enough to know that adult members of *Homo sapiens* do have such a right. For then one can conclude that any organism which belongs to the species *Homo sapiens,* from a zygote on, must also have a right to life by virtue of the potentiality principle.

The liberal, by contrast, cannot mount a comparable argument. He cannot defend his position without offering at least a partial answer to the question of what properties a thing must possess in order to have a right to life.

The importance of the potentiality principle, however, goes beyond the fact that it provides support for the conservative's position. If the principle is unacceptable, then so is his position. For if the conservative cannot defend the view that an organism's having certain potentialities is sufficient grounds for ascribing to it a right to life, his claim that a fetus which is a member of *Homo sapiens* has a right to life can be attacked as follows. The reason an adult member of *Homo sapiens* has a right to life, but an infant ape does not, is that there are certain psychological properties which the former possesses and the latter lacks. Now, even if one is unsure exactly what these psychological properties are, it is clear that an organism in the early stages of development from a zygote into an adult member of *Homo sapiens* does not possess these properties. One need merely compare a human fetus with an ape fetus. What mental states does the former enjoy that the latter does not? Surely it is reasonable to hold that there are no significant differences in their respective mental lives—assuming that one wishes to ascribe any mental states at all to such organisms. (Does a zygote have a mental life? Does it have experiences? Or beliefs? Or desires?) There are, of course, physiological differences, but these are not in themselves morally significant. *If* one held that potentialities were relevant to the ascription of a right to life, one could argue that the physiological differences, though not morally significant in themselves, are morally significant by virtue of their causal consequences: they will lead to later psychological differences that are morally relevant, and for this reason the physiological differences are themselves morally significant. But if the potentiality principle is not available, this line of argument cannot be used, and there will then be no differences between a human fetus and an ape fetus that the conservative can use as grounds for ascribing a serious right to life to the former but not to the latter.

It is therefore tempting to conclude that the conservative view of abortion is acceptable if and only if the potentiality principle is acceptable. But to say that the conservative position can be defended if the potentiality principle is acceptable is to assume that the argument is over once it is granted that the fetus has a right to life, and, as Thomson has shown there are serious grounds for questioning this assumption. In any case, the important point here is that the conservative position on abortion is acceptable *only if* the potentiality principle is sound.

One way to attack the potentiality principle is simply to argue in support of the self-consciousness requirement—the claim that only an organism that conceives of itself as a continuing subject of experience has a right to life. For this requirement, when taken together with the claim that there is at least one property, possessed by adult humans, such that any organism possessing it has a serious right to life, entails the denial of the potentiality principle. Or at least this is so if we add the uncontroversial empirical claim that an organism that will in the normal course of events develop into an adult human does not from the very beginning of its existence possess a concept of a continuing subject of experiences together with a belief that it is itself such an entity.

I think it best, however, to scrutinize the potentiality principle itself, and not to base one's case against it simply on the self-consciousness requirement. . . . The basic issue is this. Is there any property J which satisfies the following conditions: (1) There is a property K such that any individual possessing property K has a right to life, and there is a scientific law L to the effect that any organism possessing property J will in the normal course of events come to possess property K at some later time. (2) Given the relationship between property J and property K just described, anything possessing property J has a right to life. (3) If property J were not related to property K in the way indicated, it would not be the case that anything possessing property J thereby had a right to life. In short, the question is whether there is a property J that bestows a right to life on an organism *only because* J stands in a certain causal relationship to a second property K, which is such that anything possessing that property ipso facto has a right to life.

* * *

My argument against the potentiality principle can now be stated. Suppose at some future time a chemical were to be discovered which when injected into the brain of a kitten would cause the kitten to develop into a cat possessing a brain of the sort possessed by humans, and consequently into a cat having all the psychological capabilities characteristic of adult humans. Such cats would be able to think, to use language, and so on. Now it would surely be morally indefensible in such a situation to ascribe a serious right to life to members of the species Homo sapiens without also ascribing it to cats that have undergone such a process of development: there would be no morally significant differences.

Secondly, it would not be seriously wrong to refrain from injecting a newborn kitten with the special chemical, and to kill it instead. The fact that one could initiate a causal process that would transform a kitten into an entity that would eventually possess properties such that anything possessing them ipso facto has a serious right to life does not mean that the kitten has a serious right to life even before it has been subjected to the process of injection and transformation. The possibility of transforming kittens into persons will not make it any more wrong to kill newborn kittens than it is now.

Thirdly, . . . if it is not seriously wrong to refrain from initiating such a causal process, neither is it seriously wrong to interfere with such a process. Suppose a kitten is accidentally injected with the chemical. As long as it has not yet developed those properties that in themselves endow something with a right to life, there cannot be anything wrong with interfering with the causal process and preventing the development of the properties in question. Such interference might be accomplished either by injecting the kitten with some "neutralizing" chemical or simply by killing it.

But if it is not seriously wrong to destroy an injected kitten which will naturally develop the properties that bestow a right to life, neither can it be seriously wrong to destroy a member of *Homo sapiens* which lacks such properties, but will naturally come to have them. The potentialities are the same in both cases. The only difference is that in the case of a human fetus the potentialities have been present from the beginning of the organism's development, while in the case of the kitten they have been present only from the time it was injected with the special chemical. This difference in the time at which the potentialities were acquired is a morally irrelevant difference.

It should be emphasized that I am not here assuming that a human fetus does not possess properties which in themselves, and irrespective of their causal relationships to other properties, provide grounds for ascribing a right to life to whatever possesses them. The point is merely that if it is seriously wrong to kill something, the reason cannot be that the thing will later acquire properties that in themselves provide something with a right to life.

Finally, it is reasonable to believe that there are properties possessed by adult members of *Homo sapiens* which establish their right to life, and also that any normal human fetus will come to possess those properties shared by adult humans. But it has just been shown that if it is wrong to kill a human fetus, it cannot be because of its potentialities. One is therefore forced to conclude that the conservative's potentiality principle is false. . . .

VI. SUMMARY AND CONCLUSIONS

Let us return now to my basic claim, the self-consciousness requirement: An organism possesses a serious right to life only if it possesses the concept of a self as a continuing subject of experiences and other mental states, and believes that it is itself such a continuing entity. My defense of this claim has been twofold. I have offered a direct argument in support of it, and I have tried to show that traditional conservative and liberal views on abortion and infanticide, which involve a rejection of it, are unsound. I now want to mention one final reason why my claim should be accepted. Consider the example of killing, as opposed to torturing, newborn kittens. I suggest that while in the case of adult humans most people would consider it worse to kill an individual than to torture him for an hour, we do not usually view the killing of a newborn kitten as morally outrageous, although we would regard someone who tortured a newborn kitten for an hour as heinously evil. I pointed out that a possible conclusion that might be drawn from this is that newborn kittens have a right not to be tortured, but do not have a serious right to life. If this is the correct conclusion, how is one to explain it? One merit of the self-consciousness requirement is that it provides an explanation of this situation. The reason a newborn kitten does not have a right to life is explained by the fact that it does not possess the concept of a self. But how is one to explain the kitten's having a right not to be tortured? The answer is that a desire not to suffer pain can be ascribed to something without assuming that it has any concept of a continuing self. For while something that lacks the concept of a self cannot desire that a self not suffer, it can desire that a given sensation not exist. The state desired—the absence of a particular sensation, or of sensations of a certain sort—can be described in a purely phenomenalistic language, and hence without the concept of a continuing self. So long as the newborn kitten possesses the relevant phenomenal concepts, it can truly be said to desire that a certain sensation not exist. So we can ascribe to it a right not to be tortured even though, since it lacks the concept of a continuing self, we cannot ascribe to it a right to life.

This completes my discussion of the basic moral principles involved in the issue of abortion and infanticide. But I want to comment upon an important factual question, namely, at what point an organism comes to possess the concept of a self as a continuing subject of experiences and other mental states, together with the belief that it is itself such a continuing entity. This is obviously a matter for detailed psychological investigation, but everyday observation makes it perfectly clear, I believe, that a newborn baby does not possess the concept of a continuing self, any more than a newborn kitten possesses such a concept. If so, infanticide during a time interval shortly after birth must be morally acceptable.

But where is the line to be drawn? What is the cutoff point? If one maintained, as some philosophers have, that an individual possesses concepts only if he can express these concepts in language, it would be a matter of everyday observation whether or not a given organism possessed the concept of a continuing self. Infanticide would then be permissible up to the time an organism learned how to use certain expressions. However, I think the claim that acquisition of concepts is dependent on acquisition of language is mistaken. For example, one wants to ascribe mental states of a conceptual sort—such as beliefs and desires—to organisms that are incapable of learning a language. This issue of prelinguistic understanding is clearly outside the scope of this discussion. My point is simply that *if* an organism can acquire concepts without thereby acquiring a way of expressing those concepts linguistically, the question of whether a given organism possesses the concept of a self as a continuing subject of experiences and other mental states, together with the belief that it is itself such a continuing entity, may be a question that requires fairly subtle experimental techniques to answer.

If this view of the matter is roughly correct, there are two worries one is left with at the level of practical moral decisions, one of which may turn out to be deeply disturbing. The lesser worry is where the line is to be drawn in the case of infanticide. It is not troubling because there is no serious need to know the exact point at which a human infant acquires a right to life. For in the vast majority of cases in which infanticide is desirable, its desirability will be apparent within a short time after birth. Since it is virtually certain that an infant at such a stage of its development does not possess the concept of a continuing self, and thus does not possess a serious right to life, there is excellent reason to believe that infanticide is morally permissible in most cases where it is otherwise desirable. The practical moral problem can thus be satisfactorily handled by choosing some period of time, such as a week after birth, as the interval during which infanticide will be permitted. This interval could then be modified once psychologists have established the point at which a human organism comes to believe that it is a continuing subject of experiences and other mental states.

The troubling worry is whether adult animals belonging to species other than *Homo sapiens* may not also possess a serious right to life. For once one says that an organism can possess the concept of a continuing self, together with the belief that it is itself such an entity, without having any way of expressing that concept and that belief linguistically, one has to face up to the question of whether animals may not possess properties that bestow a serious right to life upon them. The suggestion itself is a familiar one, and one that most of us are accustomed to dismiss very casually. The line of thought advanced here suggests that this attitude may turn out to be tragically mistaken. Once one reflects upon the question of the *basic* moral principles involved in the ascription of a right to life to organisms, one may find himself driven to conclude that our everyday treatment of animals is morally indefensible, and that we are in fact murdering innocent persons.

NOTES

1. A clear example of such an unwillingness to entertain seriously the possibility that moral judgments widely accepted in one's own society may nevertheless be incorrect is provided by Roger Wertheimer's superficial dismissal of infanticide on pages 69-70 of his article "Understanding the Abortion Argument," *Philosophy & Public Affairs* 1, no. 1 (Fall 1971): 67-95.

2. Wertheimer, "Understanding the Abortion Argument," p. 69.

3. Ibid. p. 78

4. A moral principle accepted by a person is *basic for him* if and only if his acceptance of it is not dependent upon any of his (nonmoral) factual beliefs. That is, no change in his factual beliefs would cause him to abandon the principle in question.

5. Wertheimer, "Understanding the Abortion Argument," p. 88

6. Compare the analysis defended by Richard B. Brandt in *Ethical Theory* (Englewood Cliffs, N.J., 1950), pp. 434-441.

7. In everyday life one often speaks of desiring things, such as an apple or a newpaper. Such talk is elliptical, the context together with one's ordinary beliefs serving to make it clear that one wants to eat the apple and read the newspaper. To say that what one desires is that a certain proposition be true should not be construed as involving any particular ontological commitment. The point is merely that it is sentences such as "John wants it to be the case that he is eating an apple in the next few minutes" that provide a completely explicit description of a person's desires. If one fails to use such sentences one can be badly misled about what concepts are presupposed by a particular desire.

8. Another frequent suggestion as to the cutoff point not listed here is quickening. I omit it because it seems clear that if abortion after quickening is wrong its wrongness must be tied up with the motility of the fetus, not with mother's awareness of the fetus's ability to move about.

The Morality of Abortion

Paul Ramsey

POSSIBLE MEANINGS OF "ANIMATION"

Almost everyone has a proposal to make concerning when in the course of its prenatal or postnatal development embryonic life becomes "human." At one extreme are the views of those who hold that life is not human until the individual is a personal subject or has reason in exercise. If to be human *means* to be a person, to be a self-conscious subject of experience, or if it means to be rational, this state of affairs does not come to pass until a long while after the birth of a baby. A human infant acquires its personhood and self-conscious subjective identity through "Thou-I" encounters with other selves; and a child acquires essential rationality even more laboriously. If life must be human in these senses before it has any sanctity and respect or rights due it, infanticide would seem to be justified under any number of conditions believed to warrant it as permissible behavior or as a social policy. In any case, those who identify being human with personhood or rationality adopt a modern form of an ancient theological position called "creationism." According to this view, the unique, never-to-be-repeated individual human being (the "soul" is the religious word for him) comes into existence by a process of humanization or socialization in interaction with the persons around him. In the traditional religious language, he is "created" and "infused" into the already existing organism—sometime, gradually, after physical birth.

At the other extreme is the latest scientific view, that of modern genetics.

From James Rachels (ed.), *Moral Problems: A Collection of Philosophical Essays,* Second Edition (New York: Harper and Row Publishers, 1975), pp. 37-58. Originally appeared in Daniel Laddy, *Life or Death—Ethics and Options* (Seattle: University of Washington Press, 1971).

Indeed, microgenetics seems to have demonstrated what religion never could; and biological science, to have resolved an ancient theological dispute. The human individual comes into existence first as a minute informational speck, drawn at random from many other minute informational specks his parents possessed out of the common human gene pool. This took place at the moment of impregnation. There were, of course, an unimaginable number of combinations of specks on his paternal and maternal chromosomes that did not come to be when they were refused and he began to be. Still (with the single exception of identical twins), no one else in the entire history of the human race has ever had or will ever have exactly the same genotype. Thus, it can be said that the individual is whoever he is going to become from the moment of impregnation. Thereafter, his subsequent development may be described as a process of becoming the one he already is. Genetics teaches that we were from the beginning what we essentially still are in every cell and in every human and individual attribute. This scientific account is a modern form of the ancient theological viewpoint called "traducianism." According to this view, the unique, never-to-be-repeated individual human being (the "soul") was drawn forth from his parents at the time of conception.[1]

What is this but to say that we are all fellow fetuses? That from womb to tomb ours is a nascent life? That we are in essence congeners from the beginning? What is this but a rather antiseptic way of saying that the Creator has beset us behind and before? While we know only the light of our particular span of conscious existence, this light and that darkness whence we came and toward which we go are both alike to the One who laid his hands upon us, covered us in the womb, and by whom we were fearfully and wonderfully made.

Between the extremes of "traducianism" at conception and "creationism" gradually after birth, there are other accounts of when the human being originates and thus becomes a subject worthy of respect, rights, sanctity. No one of the positions yet to be mentioned is quite as up-to-date and scientific as the genetic account of the origin of human individuality. Among these are religious and legal viewpoints that seem always to be based on prescientific notions and "superstitions." Anglo-American law, for example, takes the moment of birth to be the moment after which there is a "man alive" (for which the evidence is air in the lungs) and before which there was no human life, separable from the mother's, that could be murdered. When it is born a "man alive," the child is from that moment already the one it ever thereafter becomes; not before, as genetics teaches. After it is born a "man alive," a child is then and then only a possible victim of the crime of "murder."

Where "abortion" is defined as a criminal offense in our legal systems, this creates another category of proscribed actions. It is not because the fetus is regarded as having sanctity or integrity or an independent right to life such as the law presupposes in the case of a "man alive." The legal reason for prohibiting abortion is not because it is believed to be a species of murder; it is the religious tradition, we shall see, and not the law which inculcates the latter view. The law's presumption is only that society has a stake in the prehuman material out of which the unique individual is to be born. Or it may be that the law exhibits a belief that as a matter of public policy society has an interest in *men* and *women*, who have an interest in and by their actions take responsibility for the prehuman material out of which an individual human being is to be brought forth a man alive.

This brings us to the theories advanced by theologians and by church-law—all doubtless to be classed, along with the law, as "superstitious" and prescientific in comparison with the genetic account of the arrival of the essential constitutive features of a human individual. The theologians propose an analysis of the prenatal development of the fetus. This means that they assert that the fetus *before* birth may be the victim of the sin of "murder." But this does not immediately entail that *all* destruction of fetal life should be classified as murder. Only modern genetics seems to lead to that conclusion, with its teaching about the unrepeatability or at least the never-to-be-repeated character of that first informational speck each of us once was and still is in every cell and attribute. Theology, however, is premicrobiology! The theologians debate the question, *when* between conception and birth the unique not-to-be-repeated individual human being has arrived on the scene. Wherever the line is drawn, the direct destruction of a fetus after that point will, by definition, be murder, while before that point its direct destruction would fall under some other species of sin or grave violation.

In the prenatal development of the fetus, "animation" is the point between conception and birth that is usually taken to be crucial, although as we shall see animation may have more than one meaning. If animation and not impregnation or birth is the moment when an individual offspring first begins to be what he is to become and launches on a course of thereafter becoming what he already is, then direct abortion after animation would be to kill a man alive. It would be—morally, not legally—a species of murder. Then, on this view, to define a direct abortion before animation as an offense would require that such an action be understood to fall within a class of less serious violations. In no case would the destruction of a preanimate fetus raise questions regarding the respect due or the rights and sanctity of another distinct human life. The fetus is then not yet human; it is still only a part of the mother's body, even though there may be a special responsibility for this prehuman material out of which is to come, at animation, a man alive.

The term "animation" may be understood in two different ways, and from this follows two different views concerning when in the course of the development of a fetus its direct abortion would be murder. "Animation" may most obviously be taken to indicate the moment fetal life becomes an independent source of movement in the womb, and modern thought would define animation in terms of physical motion. This should perhaps be called "quickening," the better to distinguish it from the second, the classical and more philosophical interpretation.

It was once commonly believed that there were forty days for the male and eighty days for the female between impregnation and the time, long before quickening, when the fetus became animate in this other sense. The second and more fundamental meaning of "animation" is derived not from motion but from *anima* (soul). The controlling philosophical doctrine was one which held that the soul is the *form of the body*. Thus *fetus animatus* = *fetus humanus* = *fetus formatus*. This did not entail another purely physical determination of when there was a formed fetus, or a fetus in human form or shape, on the scene. That would be earlier, of course, than when the fetus quickens. The meaning of the soul as the form of the body was too subtle a notion for that. It entailed a belief that there is a living human fetus, possibly much earlier than when there is either discernible motion or discernible human shape.

But the point to be noted here is that in theoretical speculation there has never been a certain or unanimous opinion among theologians to the effect that a *fetus humanus/fetus animatus* begins to be at the very moment of conception. In the controversies among theologians past and present, there has always been allowed a period of time between conception and "animation." "Scientifically" or at the level of theory or doctrine, one cannot speak with certainty of a human fetus before the lapse, some say, of six days. It is the modern science of genetics and not theology that theoretically closes this gap completely (unless segmentation in the case of identical twins is taken to be some sort of *rebutting* scientific evidence for identifying the moment of animation).

In any case, the older theologians distinguished between a formed fetus and a quickened fetus, and between nutritive, animal, and intellectual parts of the soul. They did not go so far as to say that all this was created and infused at impregnation. By the intellectual or human soul informing the fetus and by the doctrine that the soul is the "form" of the body, they meant an immanent constitutive element, not "form" in the sense of physical shape. Their reasoning entailed a distinction between *fetus formatus/fetus animatus* and a quickened fetus. This meant, of course, that the embryo became essentially human very early in its development—much earlier than could be concluded from form or animation in the gross physical senses of these terms.

In a remarkable way, modern genetics also teaches that there are "formal causes," immanent principles, or constitutive elements long before there is any shape or motion or discernible size. These minute formal elements are already determining the organic life to be the uniquely individual human being it is to be. According to this present-day scientific equivalent of the doctrine that the soul is the "form" or immanent *entelechy* of the body, it can now be asserted—not unreasonably—for the first time in the history of "scientific" speculation upon this question that who one is and is to be is present from the moment the ovum in impregnated.[2]

One can, of course, allow this and still refuse to affirm that the embryo is as yet in any sense the bearer of human rights. In that case, however, one would have to provide himself with some account (perhaps drawn from these ancient and contemporary accounts of the prenatal and postnatal developmnent of human personhood) of how by stages or degrees a human offspring approaches sacredness, and he would have to say when a child probably attains life that has sanctity. One could, for example, take "viability" and not impregnation or animation or quickening or actual birth or one year of age as the point in time when nascent life becomes subject to the protections due to any human life. Glanville Williams has recently proposed another place to draw the line, this time in between quickening and viability. "One might take," he writes, "the time at which the fetal brain begins to function," which can be determined by electrodes detecting the electric potentials or "brain waves" that are discernible in the seventh month or shortly before the time of viability, to be the beginning of justifiable protection for the fetus.[3]

Of all these demarcations, the time of birth would in many ways seem the least likely account of the beginning of life that has dignity and sanctity. A newborn baby is not noticeably much more human than before. It can, of course, do its own breathing; but before it could within limits do its own moving, and it could very definitely do its own dying. While its independence of its mother's body is relatively greater, even dramatically greater, a born baby is still a long, long way from being able to do its own praying, from being a "subject," an "I," or from being rational.

THE SANCTITY AND PROTECTION OF LIFE

Having begun with all these distinctions and theories about when germinating life becomes human, it is now necessary for me to say that from an authentic religious point of view none of them matters very much.

Strictly speaking, it is far more crucial for contemporary thought than it is for any religious viewpoint to *say when* there is on the scene enough of the actuality of a man who is coming to be for there to be any sacredness in or any rights attached to his life. This is the case because in modern world views the sanctity of life can rest only on something inherent in man. It is, therefore, important to determine when proleptically he already essentially is all else that he will ever become in the course of a long life. Respect for life in the first of it, if this has any sacredness, must be an overflow backward from or in anticipation of something—some capability or power—that comes later to be a man's inherent possession.

One grasps the religious outlook upon the sanctity of human life only if he sees that this life is asserted to be *surrounded* by sanctity that need not be in a man; that the most dignity a man ever possesses is a dignity that is alien to him. From this point of view it becomes *relatively* unimportant to say exactly when among the products of human generation we are dealing with an organism that is human and when we are dealing with organic life that is not yet human (despite all the theological speculations upon this question). A man's dignity is an overflow from God's dealings with him, and not primarily an anticipation of anything he will ever be by himself alone.

This is why in our religious traditions fetal life was so *certainly* surrounded with protections and prohibitions. This is why fetal life was surrounded by protections for the time before anyone supposed that a "man alive" *assuredly* existed, and even when, in opinions then current, there was a great degree of probability that he did not. "When nature is in delibera-tion about the man,"[4] Christians through the ages knew that God was in deliberation about the man. This took some of the weight off of analyzing the stages in the course of nature's deliberations, and off of the proofs from nature and from reason that were nevertheless used.

The value of a human life is ultimately grounded in the value God is placing on it. Anyone who can himself stand imaginatively even for a moment within an outlook where everything is referred finally to God—who, from things that are not, brings into being the things that are—should be able to see that God's deliberations about the man need have only begun. If there is anything incredible here, it is not the science, but the pitch of faith which no science proves, disproves, or confirms.

According to the religious outlooks and "on-looks" that have been traditional to us, man is a sacredness *in* human biological processes no less than he is a sacredness in the human social or political order. That sacredness is not composed by observable degrees of relative worth. A life's sanctity consists not in its worth *to* anybody. What life is in and of itself is most clearly to be seen in situations of naked equality of one life with another, and in the situation of congeneric helplessness which is the human condition in the first of life. No one is ever much more than a fellow fetus; and in order not to become confused about life's primary value, it is best not to concentrate on degrees of relative worth we may later acquire.

The Lord did not set his love upon you, nor choose you because you were already intrinsically more than a blob of tissue in the uterus or greater in size than the period at the end of this sentence. Even so, the writer of Deuteronomy proclaimed to the children of Israel:

The Lord did not set his love upon you, nor choose you, because you were more in number than any people; for you were the fewest of all people.

But because the Lord loved you, and because he would keep the oath which he had sworn unto your fathers, hath the Lord brought you out with a mighty hand . . . [7:7, 8a].

Not only the prophet Jeremiah, but anyone who has a glimmer of what it means to be a religious man, should be able to repeat after him: "Before I formed thee in the belly I knew thee; and before thou camest forth out of the womb I sanctified thee; and I ordained thee . . ." (1:5). Or after the Psalmist:

O Lord, thou hast searched me, and known me.

* * *

Thou has beset me behind and before, and laid thy hand upon me.

* * *

Behold . . . the darkness and the light are both alike to thee.
For thou hast possessed my reins:
Thou hast covered me in my mother's womb.

I will praise thee; for I am fearfully and wonderfully made: Marvelous are thy works: and that my soul knoweth right well [139:1, 5, 12b, 13, 14].

Thus, every human being is a unique, unrepeatable opportunity to praise God. His life is entirely an ordination, a loan, and a stewardship. His essence is his existence before God and to God, as it is from Him. His dignity is "an *alien* dignity," an evaluation that is not of him but placed upon him by the divine decree.

In regard to the respect to be accorded this generic, nascent, and dying life of ours, it does not matter much which of several religious formulations is chiefly invoked. This may be the doctrine concerning the origin of a human life, or man's creation in the image of God. It may be the biblical doctrine of God's covenant with his people and thence with all mankind, with the standard this provides for the mercy to be extended in every human relation. It may be the doctrine concerning man's ultimate destination. Nor does it matter much whether it is man's life from God, before God, or toward God that is most stressed in a religious philosophy of life, whether it is supernatural faith or divine charity or supernatural hope that bestows the value. In all these cases it is hardly possible to exclude what is nowadays narrowly called "nascent life" from our purview or from the blessing and sanctity and protection which—a religious man is convinced—God places over all human lives. *Sub specie Dei* human procreation is pro-creation. That is the most fundamental "pro" word in our vocabulary. This means procreation in God's behalf. *Sub specie Dei,* it was not because it could be proved that after a certain point in our pre- or even our postnatal development we became discernibly "human" and thus a bearer of rights and deserving of respect, while before that we were not; it was rather because the Lord loved us even while we were yet microscopic and sent forth his call upon us and brought forth from things that are not the things that are. *Sub specie Dei,* it is precisely the little ones who have hardly any human claims who are sought out and covered by his mercy. *Sub specie Dei,* it is precisely when all reasonable natural grounds for hope are gone that one needs hope and may hope in God, even as when all hope was gone Abraham hoped on in faith; and in this perspective it is hardly possible to exclude from the meaning of nascent life God's call sent forth among men that once again they have hope beyond and beneath the limits reason might set.

These biblical themes resound throughout Karl Barth's writings on respect for life and the protection of life. For the greatest Protestant theologian of this generation, the congeneric human situation is that ours is a "fellow humanity" held in trust. Respect for life means that a man should "treat as a loan both the life of all men with his own and his own with that of all men."5 "Respect" is indeed too pale a term to use for the attitude and response of those who "handle life as a divine loan" (p. 338). Or rather—since Barth uses the term—we must allow the word "respect" to be filled full of the meaning and awe derived from the fact that whenever a man's life is in question the primary affirmation to be made about it is that from all eternity God resolved not even to be God without this particular human life.

> Respect is man's astonishment, humility and awe at a fact in which he meets something superior—majesty, dignity, holiness, a mystery which compels him to withdraw and keep his distance, to handle it modestly, circumspectly and carefully. . . . When man in faith in God's Word and promise realized how God from eternity has maintained and loved him in his little life, and what He has done for him in time, in this knowledge of human life he is faced by a majestic, dignified and holy fact. In human life itself he meets something superior. . . . [The incarnation of Jesus Christ, the Word of God made *man*] unmistakably differentiates human life from everything that is and is done in heaven and earth. This gives it even in its most doubtful form the character of something singular, unique, unrepeatable and irreplaceable. This decides that it is an advantage and something worthwhile to be as man. This characterizes life as the incomparable and non-recurrent opportunity to praise God. [p. 339]

Respect means to treat human life with "holy awe" (p. 344).

Respect for life does not mean that a man must live and let live from some iron law of necessity, or even that there is a rational compulsion to do this, or a decisive rational ground for doing so. It is rather that because

God has said "Yes" to life, man's "Yes" should echo His. First and foremost, this means that man can and may live; he can and may respect the lives of others with his own. Into the darkness of the void before creation, or of the suicide's despair, or of a woman's womb, went forth the Divine utterance, "Thou mayest live." Because of God's decree and election, a man, in his own case, can and may live; he should ("must") accept his life as a trust superior to his own determination. Because the "can" and "may" that went forth also to summon every other life together with his own came from the same God and not from any human source, he can and may and must say the only human word that is appropriate or in accord with God's Yea-saying: "Thou, too, mayest live."

It is obviously because of this understanding of the meaning of life's sanctity that Barth can write, as it were, from above about nascent life, and not because of some pseudo science or even a correct science describing prenatal life from the underside:

> The unborn child is from the very first a child. It is still developing and has no independent life. But it is a man and not a thing, nor a mere part of the mother's body. . . . He who destroys germinating life kills a man and thus ventures the monstrous thing of decreeing concerning the life and death of a fellow-man whose life is given by God and therefore, like his own, belongs to Him. [pp. 415-416]

It is precisely because *it is only nascent* life, weak and helpless and with no intrinsic reason for claiming anything by inherent right, that Barth can say: "This child is a man for whose life the Son of God has died. . . . The true light of the world shines already in the darkness of the mother's womb" (p. 416). Or again: "Those who live by mercy will always be disposed to practice mercy, especially to a human being which is so dependent on the mercy of others as the unborn child" (p. 418).

Because it is the Lord who has beset him behind and before, the child is a bit of sacredness in the temporal and biological order—whether it is in the womb of the mother, in the arms of its father, playing hopscotch on the sidewalk, a professional football player, or a scientist at work in his laboratory (or whichever one you value most). Each has the same title to life immediately from God.

*   *   *

My final comment concerns the principal value to be derived from steadfastly maintaining the verdicts that can be reached in ethical justification or prohibition from a religious understanding of the sanctity of life and also of nascent life. This is not always or primarily the praise or blame of individual actions or agents. These may, for a variety of reasons, be *excusable* even for wrongdoing, and the judgment of blameworthiness may fall elsewhere, e.g., upon the moral ethos of an entire society or epoch. We need, therefore, to look to the fundamental moral premises of contemporary society in order to see clearly what is at stake in the survival or demise of a religious evaluation of nascent life.

This is an abortifacient society. Women readily learn to "loop before you leap," but they forget to ask whether interuterine devices prevent conception or abort germinating life. They do both. A significant part of the efficiency of the loop arises from the fact that it is not only a contraceptive, but also an abortifacient. The pills that prevent ovulation are more totally effective than the combined capacities of the loop, and this fact alone in an abortifacient civilization will lead the preference for the pill in the practice of birth control.

American women who can afford to do so go to Sweden to avail themselves of more liberal legal regulations concerning abortion;* but Swedish women go to Poland, which is at the moment the real paradise for legal abortions. Sweden's is a middle way between American rigidity and Polish unlimited permissiveness. The stated reason why Sweden does not go further and adopt still more liberal practices in regard to legal abortion is because of the fear that, as one doctor put it, where abortion is altogether easy, people will not take care to practice birth control.[6] Abortion is therefore a contraceptive device in this age. Doubtless, it is not the most choice-worthy means or a means frequently chosen, but it is an alternative means. Loop before you leap, abort before you birth! The evidence seems to be that the latter may not be merely a last resort, but is actually an option for contraceptive purposes. If quite freely available, abortion may relieve the moral and psychological pressures that are exerted upon their freedom to copulate by the remaining regard that men and women have for possible nascent life. Just as surely as this is a contraceptive society, it is also abortifacient.

We are not concerned here with what the criminal law should be in regard to abortion. Not everything that is legal is right, nor should every wrong be legally prohibited; and nothing that is right is right *because* it is legal. Perhaps the penal code regarding abortion should be reformed in directions that will lead to less evil being done than is done under our present more stringent laws.[7] However, in comprehending the meaning of describing this age as an abortifacient civilization (in contrast to societies based at all on a religious comprehension of the sanctity of life), it is illuminating to notice what happens when legal prohibitions of abortion are "liberalized." Glanville Williams[8] has this to say about the Swedish experi-

---

*It should be noted that Ramsey's essay preceded the *Roe* v. *Wade* Supreme Court decision.—Eds.

ment: "There is convincing evidence that it is to a large extent an entirely new clientele that is now granted legal abortion, that is to say women who would not have had an illegal abortion if they had been refused the legal one." Thereupon Williams states and endorses the value judgment upon these abortifacient trends that are characteristic of the contemporary period: "Although the social result is rather to add the total of legal abortions to the total of illegal abortions than to reduce the number of illegal abortions, a body of medical opinion refuses to regret the legal abortions on this account." That judgment is, of course, in no sense a "medical opinion."

The foregoing analysis of our society as in its ethos abortifacient is pertinent to the question concerning the moral justification of (direct) abortion of a fetus that is likely to be gravely defective physically or mentally. The answer to this question seems obvious indeed to a simple and sincere humanitarianism. It is not at all obvious. A first step in throwing doubt upon the proposal is to ask what was forgotten in the discussion of the blindness and deformities that will result from a woman's contracting rubella, especially in early pregnancy. It is often hard to tell whether a woman has rubella; yet her child may be gravely damaged. Moreover, it is hard to tell whether an individual case of measles is rubella; this can be determined with a great degree of certainty only in the case of *epidemics* of rubella. It is proposed that women who have rubella while pregnant should be able to secure a legal abortion, and it is affirmed that under these circumstances fetal euthanasia is not only ethically permissible but may even be morally obligatory for the sake of the child.

We are interested primarily in the ethical question. The proposal, as I understand it, is based on a kind of *interims ethik;* direct abortion is justified at least until medical science develops a *vaccine* against these measles and a reliable test of whether a woman has or has had the German measles. In our abortifacient culture, however, it is forgotten, or if mentioned it does not sink into the consciousness of men and women today, that there is an alternative to adopting the widespread medical practice and legal institution of fetal euthanasia. This optional social practice of medicine would be equally or more preventive of damage to nascent life from rubella. The *disease itself* gives complete immunization to contracting rubella again. The popular belief that a woman can have several cases of German measles is an "old wives' tale," my pediatrician tells me, which arises from the fact that it is almost impossible to tell one sort of measles from another, except in epidemics. But there is one way to be certain of this, and to obtain immunization against the disease in the future. The virus itself, the disease itself, can be used, as it were, to "vaccinate" against itself.

Why is it not proposed that for the interim between now and the perfection of a more convenient, reliable vaccine, all girl children be *given* the German measles?[9] Would this not be a more choice-worthy *interims ethik?*

The answer to this question can only be found in the complete erosion of religious regard for nascent life in a technological and abortifacient era. Abortion when the mother contracts rubella is another example of the "American way of death." In this instance, the darkness of the womb makes unnecessary resort to a morticians's art to cover the grim reality. As long as we do not see the deaths inflicted or witness the dying, the direct killing of nascent life has only to be compared with the greater or less inconvenience of other solutions in an antiseptic society where the prevention of disease at all cost is the chief light upon our conscious paths. But that darkness and this light are both alike to the Lord of nascent and conscious life. Upon this basis it would not be possible to choose actions and practices that deliberately abort over an interim social practice of deliberate disease giving. At least in the problem of rubella-induced fetal damage, it is not mercy or charity but some other motivation in regard to sentient life that can look with favor upon the practice of euthanasia for the child's sake.

The real situation in which our ethical deliberations should proceed cannot be adequately defined short of the location of moral agency and the action under consideration in the context of the lives of all mankind and the general social practices most apt to exhibit righteousness or to make for good. Moreover, our ethical deliberations cannot disregard the fact that the *specific* contemporary context must include the erosion of the moral bond between moments in a single individual life without which there can be no enduring covenants of life with life—the erosion of the moral bonds between life and life, between soul and bodily life, and between conscious life and nascent life—which has brought about the divorcing, contraceptive, and abortifacient ethos of the present day.

A chief business of ethics is to distinguish between venereal freedom and the meaning of venereal responsibility in such a fashion that it is barely possible (or at least that this possibility is not methodologically excluded) that from the reflections of moralists there may come clear direction for the structural changes needed to address the structural defects of this age. If this is so, I suggest that a strong case can be made for every effort to revitalize a religious understanding of the integrity and sanctity of life, for unfolding from this at the outmost limits the distinction between direct killing and allowing to die and the distinction between intending to kill and intending to incapacitate the fetus to save the mother's life, and for retaining in the order of ethical justification the prohibition of the direct killing of nascent life. This would be to keep needed moral pressures upon ourselves in many areas where a proper regard for life threatens to be dissolved, or has already been dissolved. This would be to endeavor to reverse the trends of a scientific and a secular age that have already gone far in emptying our culture of any substantive morality.

The first order of business would be to strengthen an ethics that contains some remaining sense of the sanctity of life against the corrosive influence of the view that what *should* be done is largely a function of what *technically can* be done, and against the view that morality is entirely a matter of engineering the consequences for the conscious span of our lives. Moreover, if we do not confuse ethical justification with moral excusability, compassion can still encompass the possibility and the reality of individual moral excusability for a wrong that had to be done or was done in a particular situation in this world where sin (especially the sin in social structures) begets sin.

NOTES

1. In order to take care of the case of identical twins (and also to account for the special ways in which our already unique combination of genetic determiners develops over a lifetime), it is necessary, of course, to bring in the modern version of "creationism" to which I have referred. Identical twins have the same genotype. They arise from the same informational speck. Yet each is and knows he is a unique, unrepeatable human person. He is something that he never was by virtue of his genes. He became something, at some time and in some manner, that he was not already, from the fission following that original conception. It is the environment who is the maker of all twin differences and the creator of a twin person's unsharable individual being; after they were born the environment "infused" this into those two blobs of identical hereditary material, which contained not only an incalculable number of powers distinguishing them as human blobs but also an incalculable number of the features of the individual beings each is to spend a whole lifetime becoming and exhibiting.

The case of identical twins does, however, suggest a significant modification of any "proof" from genotype. If we were seeking to locate a moment in the development of nascent life subsequent to impregnation and prior to birth (or graduation from Princeton) at which it would be reasonable to believe that an individual life *begins* to be inviolate, it is at least *arguable* that this takes place at the stage of *blastocyst*. In the blastocyst there appears a "primitive streak" across the hollow cluster of developing cells that signals the separation of the same genotype into identical twins. This segmentation is completed by about the time of implantation, i.e., on the seventh or eighth day after ovulation. It might be asserted that at blastocyst, not earlier, not later, these two products of human generation become "animate," each a unique individual "soul." This is *not* to say that any credit is to be given to those self-serving arguments that "implantation" is the first moment of "life" having claims upon our respect. These are, in the worst sense of the word, mere rationalizations currently offered for the purpose of rejecting out of hand the proofs that interuterine devices (the "loop") are abortifacient, and that the "morning after" or retroactive pill (which will be available in a year or so) will directly abort a human life. Still, blastocyst (which, as it happens, is roughly coincident with implantation) affords serious moralists a fact concerning nascent life (and not only concerning its location) that may and must be taken into account when dealing with the morality of using interuterine devices or a retroactive "contraceptive" pill. This may have bearing on whether the question raised by these scientific applications is one of abortion or contraception only, or of an attack upon prehuman organic matter.

2. That is, on the assumption that the morality of abortion is—at least to some degree—a science-based issue. After attributing to the present writer the view that "the biological and genetic criteria are the *only* practical way of resolving the problem," Charles E. Curran goes on to point out (with a degree of approval) that "the problem exists precisely because some people will not accept the biological and genetic criteria for *establishing* the beginning of human life" ["Natural Law and Contemporary Moral Theology," in Charles E. Curran, ed., *Contraception: Authority and Dissent* (New York: Herder and Herder, 1969), p. 164 and n. 24, italics added]. It is in place here simply to point out that one cannot arbitrarily have it both ways. One cannot appeal to those paper popes—medical and socioscientific research papers, or scientific findings in general—when in agreement with them in some matters and then disavow the relevance of biological data when one wants to mount a moral argument loosed from such considerations.

3. Glanville Williams, *The Sanctity of Life and the Criminal Law* (New York: Knopf, 1957), p. 231. On the assumption that men are *rational* animals even when they are discussing controversial moral questions and controverted public questions such as abortion, we can demand a degree of consistency between their views of when a human life begins and when a human life ends. If EEG is to determine the moment of death, EEG should be decisive in determining the moment of life's beginning. If spontaneous heartbeat still counts as a vital sign for the terminal patient, it would seem also to be a good candidate for inclusion among the vital signs of when the fetus becomes alive among us. If respiration should ever be dismissed as an indication that a brain-damaged patient is still alive, why then should respiration at birth be given such importance? If the achievement of brain and heart and lung function are all to be counted at the first of life as necessary for an individual to qualify as a being deserving respect and protection, why should not the cessation of all three be required before we cease to protect that same individual when he comes to the end of his life?

4. Tertullian, *Apologia* ix. 6-7.

5. Karl Barth, *Church Dogmatics* (Edinburg: T. and T. Clark, 1961), vol. III/4, para. 55, p. 335. All parenthetical references in the text are to this work.

6. "Abortion and the Law," CBS *Reports,* April 5, 1965.

7. Note that I say, "lead to less evil being done than is *done*," not "to less evil *happening* than now occurs." This is to say that a primary legislative purpose of law and of the reform of law in this area should remain a moral one. The goal of law is the regulation of human *conduct,* and not only the prevention of certain consequences.

8. Williams, *The Sanctity of Life,* p. 242.

9. There are sometimes, of course, serious effects from having German measles. Still, it is arguable that these effects would be far less serious than the destruction of both damaged and undamaged nascent lives which, it is said, ought now systematically to be inflicted while we await the perfection and widespread use of a vaccine.

On the Moral and Legal Status of Abortion

Mary Anne Warren

We will be concerned with both the moral status of abortion, which for our purposes we may define as the act which a woman performs in voluntarily terminating, or allowing another person to terminate, her pregnancy, and the legal status which is appropriate for this act. I will argue that, while it is not possible to produce a satisfactory defense of a woman's right to obtain an abortion without showing that a fetus is not a human being, in the morally relevant sense of that term, we ought not to conclude that the difficulties involved in determining whether or not a fetus is human make it impossible to produce any satisfactory solution to the problem of the moral status of abortion. For it is possible to show that, on the basis of intuitions which we may expect even the opponents of abortion to share, a fetus is not a person, and hence not the sort of entity to which it is proper to ascribe full moral rights.

*   *   *

The question which we must answer in order to produce a satisfactory solution to the problem of the moral status of abortion is this: How are we to define the moral community, the set of beings with full and equal moral rights, such that we can decide whether a human fetus is a member of this community or not? What sort of entity, exactly, has the inalienable rights to life, liberty, and the pursuit of happiness? Jefferson attributed these rights to all *men,* and it may or may not be fair to suggest that he intended to attribute them *only* to men. Perhaps he ought to have attributed them

From *The Monist* 57 (January 1973) pp. 43-61. Reprinted by permission of the publisher.

to all human beings. If so, then we arrive, first at [John] Noonan's problem of defining what makes a being human, and, second, at the equally vital question which Noonan does not consider, namely: What reason is there for identifying the moral community with the set of all human beings, in whatever way we have chosen to define that term?

1. ON THE DEFINITION OF 'HUMAN'

One reason why this vital second question is so frequently overlooked in the debate over the moral status of abortion is that the term 'human' has two distinct, but not often distinguished, senses. This fact results in a slide of meaning, which serves to conceal the fallaciousness of the traditional argument that since (1) it is wrong to kill innocent human beings, and (2) fetuses are innocent human beings, then (3) it is wrong to kill fetuses. For if 'human' is used in the same sense in both (1) and (2) then, whichever of the two senses is meant, one of these premises is question-begging. And if it is used in two different senses then of course the conclusion doesn't follow.

Thus, (1) is a self-evident moral truth,[1] and avoids begging the question about abortion, only if 'human being' is used to mean something like "a full-fledged member of the moral community." (It may or may not also be meant to refer exclusively to members of the species *Homo sapiens*.) We may call this the *moral* sense of 'human'. It is not to be confused with what we will call the *genetic* sense, i.e., the sense in which any member of the species is a human being, and no member of any other species could be. If (1) is acceptable only if the moral sense is intended, (2) is non-question-begging only if what is intended is the genetic sense.

In "Deciding Who is Human," Noonan argues for the classification of fetuses with human beings by pointing to the presence of the full genetic code, and the potential capacity for rational thought (p. 135). It is clear that what he needs to show, for his version of the traditional argument to be valid, is that fetuses are human in the moral sense, the sense in which it is analytically true that all human beings have full moral rights. But, in the absence of any argument showing that whatever is genetically human is also morally human, and he gives none, nothing more than genetic humanity can be demonstrated by the presence of the human genetic code. And, as we will see, the *potential* capacity for rational thought can at most show that an entity has the potential for *becoming* human in the moral sense.

2. DEFINING THE MORAL COMMUNITY

Can it be established that genetic humanity is sufficient for moral humanity? I think that there are very good reasons for not defining the moral community in this way. I would like to suggest an alternative way of defining the moral community, which I will argue for only to the extent of explaining why it is, or should be, self-evident. The suggestion is simply that the moral community consists of all and only *people,* rather than all and only human beings;[2] and probably the best way of demonstrating its self-evidence is by considering the concept of personhood, to see what sorts of entity are and are not persons, and what the decision that a being is or is not a person implies about its moral rights.

What characteristics entitle an entity to be considered a person? This is obviously not the place to attempt a complete analysis of the concept of personhood, but we do not need such a fully adequate analysis just to determine whether and why a fetus is or isn't a person. All we need is a rough and approximate list of the most basic criteria of personhood, and some idea of which, or how many, of these an entity must satisfy in order to properly be considered a person.

In searching for such criteria, it is useful to look beyond the set of people with whom we are acquainted, and ask how we would decide whether a totally alien being was a person or not. (For we have no right to assume that genetic humanity is necessary for personhood.) Imagine a space traveler who lands on an unknown planet and encounters a race of beings utterly unlike any he has ever seen or heard of. If he wants to be sure of behaving morally toward these beings, he has to somehow decide whether they are people, and hence have full moral rights, or whether they are the sort of thing which he need not feel guilty about treating as, for example, a source of food.

How should he go about making this decision? If he has some anthropological background, he might look for such things as religion, art, and the manufacturing of tools, weapons, or shelters, since these factors have been used to distinguish our human from our prehuman ancestors, in what seems to be closer to the moral than the genetic sense of 'human'. And no doubt he would be right to consider the presence of such factors as good evidence that the alien beings were people, and morally human. It would, however, be overly anthropocentric of him to take the absence of these things as adequate evidence that they were not, since we can imagine people who have progressed beyond, or evolved without ever developing, these cultural characteristics.

I suggest that the traits which are most central to the concept of personhood, or humanity in the moral sense, are, very roughly, the following:

(1) consciousness (of objects and events external and/or internal to the being), and in particular the capacity to feel pain;

(2) reasoning (the *developed* capacity to solve new and relatively complex problems);

(3) self-motivated activity (activity which is relatively independent of either genetic or direct external control);

(4) the capacity to communicate, by whatever means, messages of an indefinite variety of types, that is, not just with an indefinite number of possible contents, but on indefinitely many possible topics;

(5) the presence of self-concepts, and self-awareness, either individual or racial, or both.

Admittedly, there are apt to be a great many problems involved in formulating precise definitions of these criteria, let alone in developing universally valid behavioral criteria for deciding when they apply. But I will assume that both we and our explorer know approximately what (1)–(5) mean, and that he is also able to determine whether or not they apply. How, then, should he use his findings to decide whether or not the alien beings are people? We needn't suppose that an entity must have *all* of these attributes to be properly considered a person; (1) and (2) alone may well be sufficient for personhood, and quite probably (1)–(3) are sufficient. Neither do we need to insist that any one of these criteria is *necessary* for personhood, although once again (1) and (2) look like fairly good candidates for necessary conditions, as does (3), if 'activity' is construed so as to include the activity of reasoning.

All we need to claim, to demonstrate that a fetus is not a person is that any being which satisfies *none* of (1)–(5) is certainly not a person. I consider this claim to be so obvious that I think anyone who denied it, and claimed that a being which satisfied none of (1)–(5) was a person all the same, would thereby demonstrate that he had no notion at all of what a person is—perhaps because he had confused the concept of a person with that of genetic humanity. If the opponents of abortion were to deny the appropriateness of these five criteria, I do not know what further arguments would convince them. We would probably have to admit that our conceptual schemes were indeed irreconcilably different, and that our dispute could not be settled objectively.

I do not expect this to happen, however, since I think that the concept of a person is one which is very nearly universal (to people), and that it is common to both pro-abortionists and anti-abortionists, even though neither group has fully realized the relevance of this concept to the resolution of their dispute. Furthermore, I think that on reflection even the anti-abortionists ought to agree not only that (1)–(5) are central to the concept of personhood, but also that it is a part of this concept that all and only people have full moral rights. The concept of a person is in part a moral concept; once we have admitted that x is a person we have recognized, even if we have not agreed to respect, x's right to be treated as a member of the moral community. It is true that the claim that x is a *human being* is more commonly voiced as part of an appeal to treat x decently than is the claim that x is a person, but this is either because 'human being' is here used in the sense which implies personhood, or because the genetic and moral senses of 'human' have been confused.

Now if (1)–(5) are indeed the primary criteria of personhood, then it is clear that genetic humanity is neither necessary nor sufficient for establishing that an entity is a person. Some human beings are not people, and there may well be people who are not human beings. A man or woman whose consciousness has been permanently obliterated but who remains alive is a human being which is no longer a person; defective human beings with no appreciable mental capacity, are not and presumably never will be people; and a fetus is a human being which is not yet a person, and which therefore cannot coherently be said to have full moral rights. Citizens of the next century should be prepared to recognize highly advanced, self-aware robots or computers, should be such developed, and intelligent inhabitant of other worlds, should such be found, as people in the fullest sense, and to respect their moral rights. But to ascribe full moral rights to an entity which is not a person is as absurd as to ascribe moral obligations and responsibilities to such an entity.

3. FETAL DEVELOPMENT AND THE RIGHT TO LIFE

Two problems arise in the application of these suggestions for the definition of the moral community to the determination of the precise moral status of a human fetus. Given that the paradigm example of a person is a normal adult human being, then (1) How like this paradigm, in particular how far advanced since conception, does a human being need to be before it begins to have a right to life by virtue, not of being fully a person as of yet, but of being *like* a person? and (2) To what extent, if any, does the fact that a fetus has the *potential* for becoming a person endow it with some of the same rights? Each of these questions requires some comment.

In answering the first question, we need not attempt a detailed consideration of the moral rights of organisms which are not developed enough, aware enough, intelligent enough, etc., to be considered people, but which resemble people in some respects. It does seem reasonable to suggest that the more like a person, in the relevant respects, a being is, the stronger is the case for regarding it as having a right to life, and indeed the stronger its right to life is. Thus we ought to take seriously the suggestion that, insofar as "the human individual develops biologically in a continuous fashion . . . the rights of a human person might develop in the same way." [3] But we must keep in mind that the attributes which are relevant in determining whether or not an entity is enough like a person to be regarded as having some of the same moral rights are no different from those which are relevant to determining whether or not it is fully a person—i.e., are no different from (1)–(5)—and that being genetically human, or having recognizably human facial and other physical features, or detectable brain activity, or the capacity to survive outside the uterus, are simply not among these relevant attributes.

Thus it is clear that though a seven- or eight-month fetus has features which make it apt to arouse in us almost the same powerful protective instinct as is commonly aroused by a small infant, nevertheless it is not significantly more personlike than is a very small embryo. It is *somewhat* more personlike; it can apparently feel and respond to pain, and it may even have a rudimentary form of consciousness, insofar as its brain is quite active. Nevertheless, it seems safe to say that it is not fully conscious, in the way that an infant of a few months is, and that it cannot reason, or communicate messages of indefinitely many sorts, does not engage in self-motivated activity, and has no self-awareness. Thus, in the *relevant* respects, a fetus, even a fully developed one, is considerably less personlike than is the average mature mammal, indeed the average fish. And I think that a rational person must conclude that if the right to life of a fetus is to be based upon its resemblance to a person, then it cannot be said to have any more right to life than, let us say, a newborn guppy (which also seems to be capable of feeling pain), and that a right of that magnitude could never override a woman's right to obtain an abortion, at any stage of her pregnancy.

There may, of course, be other arguments in favor of placing legal limits upon the stage of pregnancy in which an abortion may be performed. Given the relative safety of the new techniques of artifically inducing labor during the third trimester, the danger to the woman's life or health is no longer such an argument. Neither is the fact that people tend to respond to the thought of abortion in the later stages of pregnancy with emotional repulsion, since mere emotional responses cannot take the place of moral reasoning in determining what ought to be permitted. Nor, finally, is the frequently heard argument that legalizing abortion, especially late in the pregnancy, may erode the level of respect for human life, leading, perhaps, to an increase in unjustified euthanasia and other crimes. For this threat, if it is a threat, can be better met by educating people to the kinds of moral distinctions which we are making here than by limiting access to abortion (which limitation may, in its disregard for the rights of women, be just as damaging to the level of respect for human rights).

Thus, since the fact that even a fully developed fetus is not personlike enough to have any significant right to life on the basis of its personlikeness shows that no legal restrictions upon the stage of pregnancy in which an abortion may be performed can be justified on the grounds that we should protect the rights of the older fetus; and since there is no other apparent justification for such restrictions, we may conclude that they are entirely unjustified. Whether or not it would be *indecent* (whatever that means) for a woman in her seventh month to obtain an abortion just to avoid having to postpone a trip to Europe, it would not, in itself, be *immoral,* and therefore it ought to be permitted.

4. POTENTIAL PERSONHOOD AND THE RIGHT TO LIFE

We have seen that a fetus does not resemble a person in any way which can support the claim that it has even some of the same rights. But what about its *potential,* the fact that if nurtured and allowed to develop naturally it will very probably become a person? Doesn't that alone give it at least some right to life? It is hard to deny that the fact that an entity is a potential person is a strong prima facie reason for not destroying it; but we need not conclude from this that a potential person has a right to life, by virtue of that potential. It may be that our feeling that it is better, other things being equal, not to destroy a potential person is better explained by the fact that potential people are still (felt to be) an invaluable resource, not to be lightly squandered. Surely, if every speck of dust were a potential person, we would be much less apt to conclude that every potential person has a right to become actual.

Still, we do not need to insist that a potential person has no right to life whatever. There may well be something immoral, and not just imprudent, about wantonly destroying potential people, when doing so isn't necessary to protect anyone's rights. But even if a potential person does have some prima facie right to life, such a right could not possibly outweigh the right of a woman to obtain an abortion, since the rights of any actual person invariably outweigh those of any potential person, whenever the two conflict. Since this may not be immediately obvious in the case of a human fetus, let us look at another case.

Suppose that our space explorer falls into the hands of an alien culture, whose scientists decide to create a few hundred thousand or more human beings, by breaking his body into its component cells, and using these to create fully developed human beings, with, of course, his genetic code. We may imagine that each of these newly created men will have all of the original man's abilities, skills, knowledge, and so on, and also have an individual self-concept, in short that each of them will be a bona fide (though hardly unique) person. Imagine that the whole project will take only seconds, and that its chances of success are extremely high, and that our explorer knows all of this, and also knows that these people will be treated fairly. I maintain that in such a situation he would have every right to escape if he could, and thus to deprive all of these potential people of their potential lives; for his right to life outweighs all of theirs together, in spite of the fact that they are all genetically human, all innocent, and all have a very high probability of becoming people very soon, if only he refrains from acting.

Indeed, I think he would have a right to escape even if it were not his life which the alien scientists planned to take, but only a year of his freedom, or, indeed, only a day. Nor would he be obligated to stay if he had gotten captured (thus bringing all these people-potentials into existence) because of his own carelessness, or even if he had done so deliberately, knowing the consequences. Regardless of how he got captured, he is not morally obligated to remain in captivity for *any* period of time for the sake of permitting any number of potential people to come into actuality, so great is the margin by which one actual person's right to liberty outweighs whatever right to life even a hundred thousand potential people have. And it seems reasonable to conclude that the rights of a woman will outweigh by a similar margin whatever right to life a fetus may have by virtue of its potential personhood.

Thus, neither a fetus's resemblance to a person, nor its potential for becoming a person provides any basis whatever for the claim that it has any significant right to life. Consequently, a woman's right to protect her health, happiness, freedom, and even her life, by terminating an unwanted pregnancy, will always override whatever right to life it may be appropriate to ascribe to a fetus, even a fully developed one. And thus, in the absence of any overwhelming social need for every possible child, the laws which restrict the right to obtain an abortion, or limit the period of pregnancy during which an abortion may be performed, are a wholly unjustified violation of a woman's most basic moral and constitutional rights.

NOTES

1. Of course, the principle that it is (always) wrong to kill innocent human beings is in need of many other modifications, e.g., that it may be permissible to do so to save a greater number of other innocent human beings, but we may safely ignore these complications here.

2. From here on, we will use 'human' to mean genetically human, since the moral sense seems closely connected to, and perhaps derived from, the assumption that genetic humanity is sufficient for membership in the moral community.

3. Thomas L. Hayes, "A Biological View," *Commonweal* 85 (March 17, 1967): 677-678; quoted by Daniel Callahan in *Abortion, Law, Choice, and Morality* (London: Macmillan & Co., 1970).

Abortion and the Concept of a Person

Jane English

The abortion debate rages on. Yet the two most popular positions seem to be clearly mistaken. Conservatives maintain that a human life begins at conception and that therefore abortion must be wrong because it is murder. But not all killings of humans are murders. Most notably, self-defense may justify even the killing of an innocent person.

Liberals, one the other hand, are just as mistaken in their argument that since a fetus does not become a person until birth, a woman may do whatever she pleases in and to her own body. First, you cannot do as you please with your own body if it affects other people adversely.[1] Second, if a fetus is not a person, that does not imply that you can do to it anything you wish. Animals, for example, are not persons, yet to kill or torture them for no reason at all is wrong.

At the center of the storm has been the issue of just when it is between ovulation and adulthood that a person appears on the scene. Conservatives draw the line at conception, liberals at birth. In this paper I first examine our concept of a person and conclude that no single criterion can capture the concept of a person and no sharp line can be drawn. Next I argue that if a fetus is person, abortion is still justifiable in many cases; and if a fetus is not a person, killing it is still wrong in many cases. To a large extent, these two solutions are in agreement. I conclude that our concept of a person cannot and need not bear the weight that the abortion controversy has thrust upon it.

From *Canadian Journal of Philosophy,* vol. 5, no. 2 (October 1975): pp. 233-243. Reprinted by permission of the publishers and of the author's estate.

I

The several factions in the abortion argument have drawn battle lines around various proposed criteria for determining what is and what is not a person. For example, Mary Anne Warren[2] lists five features (capacities for reasoning, self-awareness, complex communications, etc.) as her criteria for personhood and argues for the permissibility of abortion because a fetus falls outside this concept. Baruch Brody[3] uses brain waves. Michael Tooley[4] picks having-a-concept-of-self as his criterion and concludes that infanticide and abortion are justifiable, while the killing of adult animals is not. On the other side, Paul Ramsey[5] claims a certain gene structure is the defining characteristic. John Noonan[6] prefers conceived-of-humans and presents counterexamples to various other candidate criteria. For instance, he argues against viability as the criterion because the newborn and infirm would then be non-persons, since they cannot live without the aid of others. He rejects any criterion that calls upon the sorts of sentiments a being can evoke in adults on the grounds that this would allow us to exclude other races as non-persons if we could just view them sufficiently unsentimentally.

These approaches are typical: foes of abortion propose sufficient conditions for personhood which fetuses satisfy, while friends of abortion counter with necessary conditions for personhood which fetuses lack. But these both presuppose that the concept of a person can be captured in a straight-jacket of necessary and/or sufficient conditions.[7] Rather, "person" is a cluster of features, of which rationality, having a self-concept and being conceived of humans are only part.

What is typical of persons? Within our concept of a person we include, first, certain biological factors: descended from humans, having a certain genetic make-up, having a head, hands, arms, eyes, capable of locomotion, breathing, eating, sleeping. There are psychological factors: sentience, perception, having a concept of self and of one's own interests and desires, the ability to use tools, the ability to use language or symbol systems, the ability to joke, to be angry, to doubt. There are rationality factors: the ability to reason and draw conclusions, the ability to generalize and to learn from past experience, the ability to sacrifice present interests for greater gains in the future. There are social factors: the ability to work in groups and respond to peer pressures, the ability to recognize and consider as valuable the interests of others, seeing oneself as one among "other minds," the ability to sympathize, encourage, love, the ability to evoke from others the responses of sympathy, encouragement, love, the ability to work with others for mutual advantage. Then there are legal factors: being subject to the law and protected by it, having the ability to sue and enter contracts, being counted in the census, having a name and citizenship, the ability to own property, inherit, and so forth.

Now the point is not that this list is incomplete, or that you can find counterinstances to each of its points. People typically exhibit rationality, for instance, but someone who was irrational would not thereby fail to qualify as a person. On the other hand, something could exhibit the majority of these features and still fail to be a person, as an advanced robot might. There is no single core of necessary and sufficient features which we can draw upon with the assurance that they constitute what really makes a person; there are only features that are more or less typical.

This is not to say that no necessary or sufficient conditions can be given. Being alive is a necessary condition for being a person, and being a U.S. Senator is sufficient. But rather than falling inside a sufficient condition or outside a necessary one, a fetus lies in the penumbra region where our concept of a person is not so simple. For this reason I think a conclusive answer to the question whether a fetus is a person is unattainable.

Here we might note a family of simple fallacies that proceed by stating a necessary condition for personhood and showing that a fetus has that characteristic. This is a form of the fallacy of affirming the consequent. For example, some have mistakenly reasoned from the premise that a fetus is human (after all, it is a human fetus rather than, say, a canine fetus), to the conclusion that it is a human. Adding an equivocation on 'being', we get the fallacious argument that since a fetus is something both living and human, it is a human being.

Nonetheless, it does seem clear that a fetus has very few of the above family of characteristics, whereas a newborn baby exhibits a much larger proportion of them—and a two-year-old has even more. Note that one traditional anti-abortion argument has centered on pointing out the many ways in which a fetus resembles a baby. They emphasize its development ("It already has ten fingers . . . ") without mentioning its dissimilarities to adults (it still has gills and a tail). They also try to evoke the sort of sympathy on our part that we only feel toward other persons ("Never to laugh . . . or feel the sunshine?"). This all seems to be a relevant way to argue, since its purpose is to persuade us that a fetus satisfies so many of the important features on the list that it ought to be treated as a person. Also note that a fetus near the time of birth satisfies many more of these factors than a fetus in the early months of development. This could provide reason for making distinctions among the different stages of pregnancy, as the U.S. Supreme Court has done.[8]

Historically, the time at which a person had been said to come into existence has varied widely. Muslims date personhood from fourteen days after conception. Some medievals followed Aristotle in placing ensoulment at forty days after conception for a male fetus and eighty days for a female fetus.[9] In European common law since the seventeenth century, abortion was considered the killing of a person only after quickening, the time when a pregnant woman first feels the fetus move on its own. Nor is this variety of opinions surprising. Biologically, a human being develops gradually. We shouldn't expect there to be any specific time or sharp dividing point when a person appears on the scene.

For these reasons I believe our concept of a person is not sharp or decisive enough to bear the weight of a solution to the abortion controversy. To use it to solve that problem is to clarify *obscurum per obscurius*.

II

Next let us consider what follows if a fetus is a person after all. Judith Jarvis Thomson's landmark article, "A Defense of Abortion,"[10] correctly points out that some additional argumentation is needed at this point in the conservative argument to bridge the gap between the premise that a fetus is an innocent person and the conclusion that killing it is always wrong. To arrive at this conclusion, we would need the additional premise that killing an innocent person is always wrong. But killing an innocent person is sometimes permissible, most notably in self-defense. Some example may help draw out our intuitions or ordinary judgments about self-defense.

Suppose a mad scientist, for instance, hypnotized innocent people to jump out of the bushes and attack innocent passers-by with knives. If you are so attacked, we agree you have a right to kill the attacker in self-defense, if killing him is the only way to protect your life or to save yourself from serious injury. It does not seem to matter here that the attacker is not malicious but himself an innocent pawn, for your killing of him is not done in a spirit of retribution but only in self-defense.

How severe an injury may you inflict in self-defense? In part this depends upon the severity of the injury to be avoided: you may not shoot someone merely to avoid having your clothes torn. This might lead one to the mistaken conclusion that the defense may only equal the threatened injury in severity; that to avoid death you may kill, but to avoid a black eye you may only inflict a black eye or the equivalent. Rather, our laws and customs seem to say that you may create an injury somewhat, but not enormously, greater than the injury to be avoided. To fend off an attack whose outcome would be as serious as rape, a severe beating or the loss of a finger, you may shoot; to avoid having your clothes torn, you may blacken an eye.

Aside from this, the injury you may inflict should only be the minimum necessary to deter or incapacitate the attacker. Even if you know he intends to kill you, you are not justified in shooting him if you could equally well save yourself by the simple expedient of running away. Self-defense is for the purpose of avoiding harms rather than equalizing harms.

Some cases of pregnancy present a parallel situation. Though the fetus is itself innocent, it may pose a threat to the pregnant woman's well-being, life prospects or health, mental or physical. If the pregnancy presents a slight threat to her interests, it seems self-defense cannot justify abortion. But if the threat is on a par with a serious beating or the loss of a finger, she may kill the fetus that poses such a threat, even if it is an innocent person. If a lesser harm to the fetus could have the same defensive effect, killing it would not be justified. It is unfortunate that the only way to free the woman from the pregnancy entails the death of the fetus (except in very late stages of pregnancy). Thus a self-defense model supports Thomson's point that the woman has a right only to be freed from the fetus, not a right to demand its death.[11]

The self-defense model is most helpful when we take the pregnant woman's point of view. In the pre-Thomson literature, abortion is often framed as a question for a third party: do you, a doctor, have a right to choose between the life of the woman and that of the fetus? Some have claimed that if you were a passer-by who witnessed a struggle between the innocent hypnotized attacker and his equally innocent hypnotized victim, you would have no reason to kill either in defense of the other. They have concluded that the self-defense model implies that a woman may attempt to abort herself, but that a doctor should not assist her. I think the position of the third party is somewhat more complex. We do feel some inclination to intervene on behalf of the victim rather than the attacker, other things equal. But if both parties are innocent, other factors come into consideration. You would rush to the aid of your husband whether he was attacker or attackee. If a hypnotized famous violinist were attacking a skid row bum, we would try to save the individual who is of more value to society. These considerations would tend to support abortion in some cases.

But suppose you are a frail senior citizen who wishes to avoid being knifed by one of these innocent hypnotics, so you have hired a bodyguard to accompany you. If you are attacked, it is clear we believe that the bodyguard, acting as your agent, has a right to kill the attacker to save you from a serious beating. Your rights of self-defense are transferred to your agent. I suggest that we should similarly view the doctor as the pregnant woman's agent in carrying out a defense she is physically incapable of accomplishing herself.

Thanks to modern technology, the cases are rare in which a pregnancy poses as clear a threat to a woman's bodily health as an attacker brandishing a switchblade. How does self-defense fare when more subtle, complex, and long-range harms are involved?

To consider a somewhat fanciful example, suppose you are a highly trained surgeon when you are kidnapped by the hypnotic attacker. He says he does not intend to harm you but to take you back to the mad scientist who, it turns out, plans to hypnotize you to have a permanent mental block against all your knowledge of medicine. This would automatically destroy your career which would in turn have a serious adverse impact on your family, your personal relationships and your happiness. It seems to me that if the only way you can avoid this outcome is to shoot the innocent attacker, you are justified in so doing. You are defending yourself from a drastic injury to your life prospects. I think it is no exaggeration to claim that unwanted pregnancies (most obviously among teenagers) often have such adverse life-long consequences as the surgeon's loss of livelihood.

Several parallels arise between various views on abortion and the self-defense model. Let's suppose further that these hypnotized attackers only operate at night, so that it is well known that they can be avoided completely by the considerable inconvenience of never leaving your house after dark. One view is that since you could stay home at night, therefore if you go out and are selected by one of these hypnotized people, you have no right to defend yourself. This parallels the view that abstinence is the only acceptable way to avoid pregnancy. Others might hold that you ought to take along some defense such as Mace which will deter the hypnotized person without killing him, but that if this defense fails, you are obliged to submit to the resulting injury, no matter how severe it is. This parallels the view that contraception is all right but abortion is always wrong, even in cases of contraceptive failure.

A third view is that you may kill the hypnotized person only if he will actually kill you, but not if he will only injure you. This is like the position that abortion is permissible only if it is required to save a woman's life. Finally we have the view that it is all right to kill the attacker, even if only to avoid a very slight inconvenience to yourself and even if you knowingly walked down the very street where all these incidents have been taking place without taking along any Mace or protective escort. If we assume that a fetus is a person, this is the analogue of the view that abortion is always justifiable, "on demand."

The self-defense model allows us to see an important difference that exists between abortion and infanticide, even if a fetus is a person from conception. Many have argued that the only way to justify abortion without justifying infanticide would be to find some characteristic of personhood that is acquired at birth. Michael Tooley, for one, claims infanticide is justifiable because the really significant characteristics of person are acquired some time after birth. But all such approaches look to characteristics of the developing human and ignore the relation between the fetus and the woman. What if, after birth, the presence of an infant or the need to support it posed a grave threat to the woman's sanity or life prospects? She could escape this treat by the simple expedient of running away. So a solution that does not entail the death of the infant is available. Before birth, such solutions are not available because of the biological dependence of the fetus on the woman. Birth is the crucial point not because of any characteristics the fetus gains, but because after birth the woman can defend herself by a means less drastic than killing the infant. Hence self-defense can be used to justify abortion without necessarily thereby justifying infanticide.

III

On the other hand, supposing a fetus is not after all a person, would abortion always be morally permissible? Some opponents of abortion seem worried that if a fetus is not a full-fledged person, then we are justified in treating it in any way at all. However, this does not follow. Non-persons do get some consideration in our moral code, though of course they do not have the same rights as persons have (and in general they do not have moral responsibilities), and though their interests may be overridden by the interests of persons. Still, we cannot just treat them in any way at all.

Treatment of animals is a case in point. It is wrong to torture dogs for fun or to kill wild birds for no reason at all. It is wrong Period, even though dogs and birds do not have the same rights persons do. However, few people think it is wrong to use dogs as experimental animals, causing them considerable suffering in some cases, provided that the resulting research will probably bring discoveries of great benefit to people. And most of us think it all right to kill birds for food or to protect our crops. People's rights are different from the consideration we give to animals, then, for it is wrong to experiment on people, even if others might later benefit a great deal as a result of their suffering. You might volunteer to be a subject, but this would be supererogatory; you certainly have a right to refuse to be a medical guinea pig.

But how do we decide what you may or may not do to non-persons? This is a difficult problem, one for which I believe no adequate account exists. You do not want to say, for instance, that torturing dogs is all right whenever the sum of its effects on people is good—when it doesn't warp the sensibilities of the torturer so much that he mistreats people. If that were the case, it would be all right to torture dogs if you did it in private, or if the torturer lived on a desert island or died soon afterward, so that his actions had no effect on people. This is an inadequate account, because whatever moral consideration animals get, it has to be indefeasible, too. It will have to be a general proscription of certain actions, not merely a weighing of the impact on people on a case-by-case basis.

Rather, we need to distinguish two levels on which consequences of actions can be taken into account in moral reasoning. The traditional objections to Utilitarianism focus on the fact that it operates solely on the first level, taking all the consequences into account in particular cases only.

Thus Utilitarianism is open to "desert island" and "lifeboat" counterexamples because these cases are rigged to make the consequences of actions severely limited.

Rawls's theory could be described as a teleological sort of theory, but with teleology operating on a higher level.[12] In choosing the principles to regulate society from the original position, his hypothetical choosers make their decision on the basis of the total consequences of various systems. Furthermore, they are constrained to choose a general set of rules which people can readily learn and apply. An ethical theory must operate by generating a set of sympathies and attitudes toward others which reinforce the functioning of that set of moral principles. Our prohibition against killing people operates by means of certain moral sentiments including sympathy, compassion, and guilt. But if these attitudes are to form a coherent set, they carry us further: we tend to perform supererogatory actions, and we tend to feel similar compassion toward person-like non-persons.

It is crucial that psychological facts play a role here. Our psychological constitution makes it the case that for our ethical theory to work, it must prohibit certain treatment of non-persons which are significantly person-like. If our moral rules allowed people to treat some personlike non-persons in ways we do not want people to be treated, this would undermine the system of sympathies and attitudes that makes the ethical system work. For this reason, we would choose in the original position to make mistreatment of some sorts of animals wrong in general (not just wrong in the cases with public impact), even though animals are not themselves parties in the original position. Thus it makes sense that it is those animals whose appearance and behavior are most like those of people that get the most consideration in our moral scheme.

It is because of "coherence of attitudes," I think, that the similarity of a fetus to a baby is very significant. A fetus one week before birth is so much like a newborn baby in our psychological space that we cannot allow any cavalier treatment of the former while expecting full sympathy and nurturative support for the latter. Thus, I think that anti-abortion forces are indeed giving their strongest arguments when they point to the similarities between a fetus and a baby, and when they try to evoke our emotional attachment to and sympathy for the fetus. An early horror story from New York about nurses who were expected to alternate between caring for six-week premature infants and disposing of viable 24-week aborted fetuses is just that—a horror story. These beings are so much alike that no one can be asked to draw a distinction and treat them so very differently.

Remember, however, that in the early weeks after conception, a fetus is very much unlike a person. It is hard to develop these feelings for a set of genes which doesn't yet have a head, hands, beating heart, response to touch or the ability to move by itself. Thus it seems to me that the alleged "slippery slope" between conception and birth is not so very slippery. In the early stages of pregnancy, abortion can hardly be compared to murder for psychological reasons, but in the latest stages it is psychologically akin to murder.

Another source of similarity is the bodily continuity between fetus and adult. Bodies play a surprisingly central role in our attitudes toward persons. One has only to think of the philosophical literature on how far physical identity suffices for personal identity or Wittgenstein's remark that the best picture of the human soul is the human body. Even after death, when all agree the body is no longer a person, we still observe elaborate customs of respect for the human body; like people who torture dogs, necrophiliacs are not to be trusted with people.[13] So it is appropriate that we show respect to a fetus as the body continuous with the body of a person. This is a degree of resemblance to persons that animals cannot rival.

Michael Tooley also utilizes a parallel with animals. He claims that it is always permissible to drown newborn kittens and draws conclusions about infanticide.[14] But it is only permissible to drown kittens when their survival would cause some hardship. Perhaps it would be a burden to feed and house six more cats or to find other homes for them. The alternative of letting them starve produces even more suffering than the drowning. Since the kittens get their rights secondhand, so to speak, *via* the need for coherence in our attitudes, their interests are often overriden by the interests of full-fledged persons. But if their survival would be no inconvenience to people at all, then it is wrong to drown them, *contra* Tooley.

Tooley's conclusions about abortion are wrong for the same reason. Even if a fetus is not a person, abortion is not always permissible, because of the resemblance of a fetus to a person. I agree with Thomson that it would be wrong for a woman who is seven months pregnant to have an abortion just to avoid having to postpone a trip to Europe. In the early months of pregnancy when the fetus hardly resembles a baby at all, then, abortion is permissible whenever it is in the interests of the pregnant woman or her family. The reasons would only need to outweigh the pain and inconvenience of the abortion itself. In the middle months, when the fetus comes to resemble a person, abortion would be justifiable only when the continuation of the pregnancy or the birth of the child would cause harms—physical, psychological, economic or social—to the woman. In the late months of pregnancy, even on our current assumption that a fetus is not a person, abortion seems to be wrong except to save a woman from significant injury or death.

The Supreme Court has recognized similar gradations in the alleged slippery slope stretching between conception and birth. To this point, the present paper has been a discussion of the moral status of abortion only, not its legal status. In view of the great physical, financial and sometimes psychological costs of abortion, perhaps the legal arrangement most compatible with the proposed moral solution would be the absence of restrictions, that is, so-called abortion "on demand."

So I conclude, first, that application of our concept of a person will not suffice to settle the abortion issue. After all, the biological development of a human being is gradual. Second, whether a fetus is a person or not, abortion is justifiable early in pregnancy to avoid modest harms and seldom justifiable late in pregnancy except to avoid significant injury or death.

NOTES

1. We also have paternalistic laws which keep us from harming our own bodies even when no one else is affected. Ironically, anti-abortion laws were originally designed to protect pregnant women from a dangerous but tempting procedure.

2. Mary Anne Warren, "On the Moral and Legal Status of Abortion," *Monist* 5 (1973), p. 55. [See this volume, pp. 75-82.]

3. Baruch Brody, "Fetal Humanity and the Theory of Essentialism," in Robert Baker and Frederick Elliston (eds.), *Philosophy and Sex* (Buffalo, N.Y., 1975).

4. Michael Tooley, "Abortion and Infanticide," *Philosophy and Public Affairs* 1 (1971). [See this volume, pp. 45-60.]

5. Paul Ramsey, "The Morality of Abortion," in James Rachels, ed., *Moral Problems* (New York, 1971). [See this volume pp. 61-74.]

6. John Noonan, "Abortion and the Catholic Church: a Summary History," *Natural Law Forum* 12 (1967):125-131.

7. Wittgenstein has argued against the possibility of so capturing the concept of a game, *Philosophical Investigations* (New York, 1958), §66-71.

8. Not because the fetus is partly a person and so has some of the rights of persons but rather because of the rights of personlike non-persons. This I discuss in part III below.

9. Aristotle himself was concerned, however, with the different question of when the soul takes form. For historical data, see Jimmye Kimmey, "How the Abortion Laws Happened," *Ms.* 1 (April, 1973):48ff and John Noonan, *loc. cit.*

10. J. J. Thomson, " A Defense of Abortion," *Philosophy and Public Affairs* 1 (1971). [See this volume pp. 29-44.]

11. Ibid., [32-33, 43-44].

12. John Rawls, *A Theory of Justice* (Cambridge, Mass., 1971), §3-4.

13. On the other hand, if they can be trusted with people, then our moral customs are mistaken. It all depends on the facts of psychology.

14. Tooley, op. cit., p. [56].

An Appeal for Consistency

Harry J. Gensler

If you asked ten years ago for my view on the morality of abortion, I would have said "I don't have a view—the issue confuses me." But now I think that abortion is wrong and that certain Kantian consistency requirements more or less force us into thinking this. Part III will present my reasoning. But first, in Parts I and II, I will show why various traditional and recent arguments on abortion do not work.

I. A TRADITIONAL ANTI-ABORTION ARGUMENT

One common traditional argument goes this way:

> The killing of innocent human life is wrong.
>
> The fetus is innocent human life.
>
> Therefore, the killing of the fetus is wrong.

This seemingly simple argument raises some difficult questions:

> It is "always wrong" or "normally wrong"? And if the latter, how do we decide the difficult cases?
>
> Is the fetus "innocent" if it is attacking the life or health or social well-being of the woman?

From "A Kantian Argument Against Abortion,"*Philosophical Studies* No. 49 (1986): 83-98. Reprinted by permission of Kluwer Academic Publishers.

Is there a clear and morally-weighty distinction between "killing" and "letting die"—or between "direct killing" and "indirect killing"?

I will not discuss these important questions; a short essay on abortion must leave many questions unanswered. But I will discuss this one: "What does the term 'human life' in the abortion argument mean?" People sometimes presume that the meaning of the term is clear and that the major problem is the factual one of whether the fetus is "human life" (in some clear sense). But I think that the term in this context is fuzzy and could be used in different senses.

Suppose we found a Martian who could discuss philosophy; would he be "human"? We need to make distinctions: the Martian would be "human" in the sense of "animal capable of reasoning" ("rational animal") but not in the sense of "member of the species *Homo sapiens*"—so the Martian is "human" in one sense but not in another. Which of these senses should be used in the abortion argument? The fetus is not yet an "animal capable of reasoning." Is it a "member of the species *Homo sapiens*"? That depends on whether the unborn are to be counted as "members" of a species—ordinary language can use the term either way. In the biology lab we all (regardless of our views on abortion) distinguish between "human" fetuses and "mouse" fetuses—so in this sense (the "genetic sense") the fetus is human. But in counting the number of mice or humans in the city of Chicago we all (regardless of our views on abortion) count only the born—so in this sense ("the population-study sense") the fetus is not a human. So is the fetus a "human"? In two senses of this term that we have distinguished the answer would be NO while in a third sense the answer would be YES; whether the fetus is "human" depends on what is meant by "human."

Human life has been claimed to begin at various points:

(1) at conception.

(2) when individuality is assured (and the zygote cannot split or fuse with another).

(3) when the fetus exhibits brain waves.

(4) when the fetus could live apart.

(5) at birth.

(6) when the being becomes self-conscious and rational.

Here we do not have a factual disagreement over when there emerges, in the same clear sense of the term, a "human"; rather we have six ways to use the term. Answer (1) is correct for the "genetic sense," (5) for the "population-study sense," and (6) for the "rational animal sense"; answers (2) to

(4) reflect other (possibly idiosyncratic) senses. And there are likely other senses of "human" besides these six. Which of these are we to use in the first premise ("The killing of innocent *human* life is wrong")? We get different principles depending on which sense of the term "human" we use.

Can we decide which sense to use by appealing to scientific data? No, we cannot. Scientific data can help us judge whether a specific individual is "human" in some specified sense (e.g., sense [3] or sense [4]) but it cannot tell us which sense of "human" to use in our principle.

Can we decide by "intuition"—by following the principle that *seems* most correct? Note that moral intuitions depend greatly on upbringing and social milieu. Most Catholics were brought up to have intuitions in line with sense (1) (the "genetic sense"). Many ancient Romans and Greeks were trained to have sense (6) intuitions (allowing abortion *and* infanticide). And many Americans today are being brought up to have sense (5) intuitions (allowing abortion but not infanticide). Is there any way to resolve this clash—other than simply praising our own intuitions and insulting contrary ones? Can we carry on the argument further? I think we can and that the Kantian appeal to consistency provides a way to resolve the issue rationally.

II. SOME RECENT PRO-ABORTION ARGUMENTS

Before getting to the Kantian approach, let us consider three arguments in defense of abortion. A common utilitarian argument goes this way:

> Anything having a balance of good results (considering everyone) is morally permissible.
>
> Abortion often has a balance of good results (considering everyone).
>
> Therefore, abortion often is morally permissible.

Here "good results" is most commonly interpreted in terms of pleasure and pain ("hedonistic act utilitarianism") or the satisfaction of desires ("preference act utilitarianism").

The second premise (on the good results of abortion) is controversial. People defending the premise say that abortion often avoids difficulties such as the financial burden of a child on poor parents or on society, the disruption of schooling or a career, and the disgrace of an unwed mother; that where these problems or probable birth defects exist, the child-to-be would have less chance for happiness; and that abortion provides a "second chance" to prevent a birth when contraceptives fail or people want to rethink an earlier choice. But opponents say that we can have equally good results without abortion, by using better social structures (more social support toward unwed mothers and poor families, better adoption practices, wiser use of contraceptives, etc.) and scientific advances (better contraceptives, artificial wombs, etc.); and they say that abortion can harm the woman psychologically and promote callous attitudes toward human life.

I think the weaker link is the first premise—the argument's utilitarian basis. This premise would often justify killing, not just fetuses, but also infants and the sick or handicapped or elderly; many utilitarian reasons for not wanting a child around the house would also apply to not wanting grandmother around. And the premise would justify these killings, not just when they have great utilitarian benefits, but even when the utilitarian benefits are slight. Utilitarian says that the killing of an innocent human being is justified whenever it brings even a slight increase in the sum-total of pleasure (or desire-satisfaction). This is truly bizarre.

Imagine a town where lynchings give the people pleasure (or satisfy their desires) and the utilitarian sheriff lynches an innocent person each week because the pleasure (or desire) of the masses slightly outweighs the misery (or frustration of desire) of the person to be lynched—and so the action has a slight gain in "good results." If the utilitarian principle is correct then the sheriff's lynchings are morally justified! But could anyone really believe that these lynchings would be morally justified?

I could pile up further examples of strange and unbelievable implications of utilitarianism. Utilitarians try to weasel out of these examples but I think not with ultimate success. So my verdict on utilitarianism is that it would justify so many bizarre actions (including so many killings) that we would not accept this principle if we were consistent and realized its logical consequences.

My second pro-abortion argument is from Michael Tooley.[1] Tooley recognizes that humans have a right to life—presumably a greater right than utilitarians would recognize; but only humans in sense (6) ("rational animals"—or, as he puts it, "persons") have such a right. The human fetus, while it might develop into a being with a right to life, presently has no more right to life than a mouse fetus. A fetus lacks a right to life because "rights" connect with "desires" conceptually—so that you can have rights only if you have desires. Tooley's argument is roughly this:

A being has a right to X only if it desires X.

No fetus desires its continued existence [because then the fetus would have to have a concept of itself as a continuing subject of experiences— a concept it cannot as yet have].

Therefore, no fetus has a right to its continued existence.

Tooley claims that the first premise is not correct as it stands; we must add three qualifications to make the premise harmonize with our intuitions regarding rights:

> A being has a right to X only if either it desires X or else it would desire X were it not (a) emotionally unbalanced or (b) temporarily unconscious or (c) conditioned otherwise.

He thinks the revised first premise will serve equally well (assuming obvious changes in the second premise); so he concludes that fetuses (and infants) do not have a right to life.

But we need further exceptions to make the first premise correspond to our intuitions. If we think that the dead have rights (e.g., to have their wills followed), then we need to add "or (d) the being did desire X when it was alive." If we think that a child who lacks the concept "hepatitis" (and thus cannot desire not to be given this disease) does not thereby lose his right not to be given hepatitis, then we need to add "or (e) the being would desire X if it had the necessary concepts." If we think (as I do) that trees and canyons have the right not to be destroyed without good reason, then we would have to add some exception for this. And if we think that the fetus (or infant) has a right to life, then we need to add something like "or (f) if the being were to grow up to be an adult member of the rational species to which it belongs then it would desire to have had X" (presumably if the fetus were to grow up to be an adult member of *Homo sapiens* then it would desire to have had continued life—and this, with (f), allows the fetus to have a right to life).[2] The trouble with Tooley's argument is that disagreements over the main issue of the right to life of the fetus translate into disagreements over how to qualify the first premise to make it mesh with "our" intuitions; so the argument cannot decide the main issue.

The third argument in defense of abortion comes from Judith Jarvis Thomson and presumes that the fetus is a "person" (in some undefined sense):[3]

> One who has voluntarily assumed no special obligation toward another person has no obligation to do anything requiring great personal cost to preserve the life of the other.

> Often a pregnant woman has voluntarily assumed no special obligation toward the unborn child (a person), and to preserve its life by continuing to bear the unborn child would require great personal cost.

> Therefore, often a pregnant woman has no obligation to continue to bear the unborn child.

The first premise here seems acceptable. Normally you have no obligation to risk your life to save a drowning stranger; if you risk your life then you do more than duty requires. But it is different if you are a lifeguard who has assumed a special obligation—then you have to try to save the person, even at the risk of your own life. Thomson thinks that a woman getting pregnant intending to have a child is voluntarily accepting a special obligation toward the child. However if the pregnancy is accidental (the result of a contraceptive failure or rape) then the woman has assumed no such special obligation and, if continuing to bear the child requires great personal cost, the woman has no obligation to continue to bear it; the woman would do no wrong if she has an abortion—but if she continues to bear the child in spite of personal cost then she is doing something heroic, something beyond what duty requires.

Thomson gives an analogy. Suppose you wake up and find yourself in bed with an unconscious violinist attached to your circulatory system (his friends attached him to you because this was needed to save his life); if you disconnect him before nine months, he will die—otherwise he will live. Even though it might be praiseworthy to make the sacrifice and leave him plugged in for nine months, still you have no obligation to do so; it would be morally right for you to disconnect him, even though he will die. So also if you are pregnant under the conditions mentioned above, then, even though it might be praiseworthy to make the sacrifice and bear the child for nine months, still you have no obligation to do so; it would be morally right for you to have the child removed, even though it will die.

The first premise of Thomson's argument is slightly misstated. A motorist has a special obligation toward a person he has injured in an accident, even though he has not voluntarily assumed this obligation in any clear way (the accident happened against his will and despite all reasonable precautions—just like an accidental pregnancy). Similarly a child has a special obligation towards his parents—even though he has not voluntarily assumed this obligation. Not all special obligations toward others are "voluntarily assumed"—so these two words should be crossed out in the premises.

My main objection to the argument can be put as a dilemma. Utilitarianism is either true or false. If it is *true,* then the first premise is false (because then the person has an obligation to do whatever has the best consequences—despite personal cost); and so the pro-abortion utilitarian Peter Singer rejects this premise, since it conflicts with utilitarianism. But if utilitarianism is *false,* then presumably Sir David Ross was right in claiming it to be morally significant that others:

> . . . stand to me in relation of promisee to promiser, of creditor to debtor, of wife to husband, *of child to parent* [my emphasis], of friend to friend, of fellow countryman to fellow countryman, and the like; and each of these

relations is the foundation of a *prima facie* duty, which is more or less incumbent on me according to the circumstances of the case.[4]

If utilitarianism is *false,* then likely a person has greater obligations toward his or her offspring than toward a violinist stranger—and so the second premise, which claims that the pregnant woman has no special responsibility toward her own child, begins to look doubtful (recall that we crossed out the words "voluntarily assumed").

III. A KANTIAN ARGUMENT

My Kantian approach to abortion stresses consistency. In discussing utilitarianism I appealed to simple logical consistency (not accepting a principle without accepting its recognized logical consequences). Here I will use two further consistency requirements (based on the universalizability and prescriptivity principles) and a third consistency requirement derived from these two (a version of the golden rule). The following argument displays these three requirements and how the third follows form the first two:

> If you are consistent and think that it would be all right for someone *to do A to X,* then you will think that it would be all right for someone *to do A to you* in similar circumstances.

> If you are consistent and think that it would be *all right* for someone to do *A* to you in similar circumstances, then you will *consent* to the idea of someone doing *A* to you in similar circumstances.

> Therefore, if you are consistent and think that it would be *all right to do A to X,* then you will *consent* to the idea of someone *doing A to you* in similar circumstances. (GR)

The first premise can be justified by the "universalizability principle," which demands that we make similar ethical judgments about the same sort of situation (regardless of the individuals involved); so if I think it would be all right to rob *Jones* but I don't think it would be all right for someone to rob *me* in an imagined exactly similar situation, then I violate universalizability and am inconsistent. The second premise can be justified by the "prescriptivity principle," which demands that we keep our ethical beliefs in harmony with the rest of our lives (our actions, intentions, desires, and so forth); so if I think an act would be all right but I don't consent to it being done, then I violate prescriptivity and am inconsistent. These and further derived requirements can be formulated and justified in a rigorous way; but I won't do that here. The conclusion GR is a form of the golden rule; if I think it would be all right to rob Jones but yet I don't consent to (or approve of) the idea of someone robbing me in similar circumstances, then I violate GR and am inconsistent.[5]

The following argument combines an instance of GR with an empirical premise about your desires:

> If you are consistent and think that *stealing is normally permissible,* then you will consent to the idea of *people stealing from you* in normal circumstances. (From GR)
>
> You do not consent to the idea of people stealing from you in normal circumstances.
>
> Therefore, if you are consistent then you will not think that stealing is normally permissible.

Most of us do not consent to the idea of people stealing from us in normal circumstances; so we would not be consistent if we held "Stealing is normally permissible" (since then we would violate consistency principle GR). This argument shows that, given that a person has a certain desire (one that most people can be presumed to have), he would not be consistent if he held a given ethical view. The conclusion here concerns the consistency of holding the ethical judgment and not the judgment's truth. A person could escape this conclusion if he did not care if people robbed him; then the second premise would be false. Throughout the rest of this essay I will generally assume that the reader desires not to be robbed or blinded or killed; if you would love people to rob or blind or kill you (or you don't care whether they do this to you)—then most of my further conclusions will not apply to you.

It might seem easy to argue similarly on abortion. How would you like it if someone had aborted you? Should we say that you don't like the idea and so you can't consistently hold that abortion is permissble? Or should we say that as an ignorant fetus you would not have known enough to have been against the abortion—so that this argument won't work?

Let us slow down and try to understand GR more clearly before applying it to abortion. Properly understood, GR has to do with my *present reaction* toward a hypothetical case—not with how I *would react if I were* in the hypothetical case. A few examples may clarify things. Consider this chart:

Issue	*Right Question*	*Wrong Question*
Do I think it permissible to rob X while X is asleep?	Do I now consent to the idea of my being robbed while asleep?	If I were robbed while I was asleep would I then (while asleep) consent to this action?

(In the "Right Question" and "Wrong Question" I presume implicit "in relevantly or exactly similar circumstances" qualifiers). The point of this chart is that, by GR, to be consistent in answering YES to the ISSUE I must also answer *yes* to the *right question*—but I need not answer *yes* to the *wrong question*. Presumably I would answer *no* to the *right questions;* when I consider the hypothetical case of my-being-robbed-while asleep. I find that I now (while awake) do not consent to or approve of this action. But the *wrong question* has to do with what I, if I were robbed while asleep, would consent to or approve of while thus asleep (and thus ignorant of the robbery); GR, correctly understood, has nothing to do with the *wrong question*. Let me give another example:

Issue	Right Question	Wrong Question
Do I think it permissible to violate *X's* will after his death?	Do I now consent to the idea of my will being violated after my death?	If my will is violated after my death, would I then (while dead) consent to this action?

Again GR has to do with my *present reaction* toward a hypothetical case in which I may imagine myself as asleep or dead or even a fetus—but not with how I *would* react *while* asleep or dead or a fetus *in* the hypothetical situation.

But is it legitimate to apply the golden rule to our treatment of a fetus? Consider a case not involving abortion:

Issue	Right Question	Wrong Question
Do I think it permissible to blind *X* while *X* is a fetus?	Do I now consent to the idea of my having been blinded while a fetus?	If I were blinded while a fetus, would I then (while a fetus) consent to this action?

Suppose that you had a sadistic mother who, while pregnant with you, contemplated injecting herself with a blindness-drug which would have no effect on her but which would cause the fetus (you) to be born blind an remain blind all its (your) life. Your mother could have done this to you. Do you think this would have been all right—and do you consent to the idea of her having done this? The answer is a clear *no*—and an equally clear *no* regardless of the time of pregnancy that we imagine the injection taking place. We could then argue as we did concerning stealing:

If you are consistent and think that *blinding a fetus is normally permissible,* then you will consent to the idea of *your having been blinded while a fetus* in normal circumstances. (From GR)

You do not consent to the idea of your having been blinded while a fetus in normal circumstances.

Therefore, if you are consistent then you will not think that blinding a fetus is normally permissible.

Again, with most people the second premise will be true—most people can be presumed not to consent to (or approve of) the idea of this act having been done to them.

It is legitimate to apply the golden rule to our treatment of a fetus? Surely it is—the above reasoning makes good sensse. If a pregnant woman is about to do something harmful to the fetus (like taking drugs or excessive alcohol or cigarettes), it seems appropriate for her to ask, "How do I now react to the idea of my mother having done this same thing while she was pregnant with me?" Applying the golden rule to a fetus raises no special problems.

But someone might object as follows:

Seemingly your view forces us to accept that the fetus has rights (e.g., not to be blinded by the drug), even though you avoid saying it is human. But your question about "*my* having been blinded *while a fetus*" presupposes that the fetus and my present self are identical—the *same human being.* So aren't you presupposing (despite your earlier discussion on the many senses of "human") that the fetus is "human"?

While my way of phrasing the question may presuppose this, I put my question this way only for the sake of convenience; I could rephrase my question so that it doesn't presuppose this:

Do I now consent to the idea of:

— my having been blinded while a fetus?

— the fetus that developed into my present self having been blinded?

— Helen E. Gensler having taken the blindness-drug while pregnant in 1945?

The second and third way to phrase the question do not presuppose that the fetus and my present self are identical or the same human being; if you wish, you may rephrase my comments thusly (I will keep to the first way of speaking for the sake of brevity). I am against the idea of the drug having been given, not because I think that the fetus was in some metaphysical sense the *same human being* as I, but rather because if this drug had been given then I would be blind all my life.

The application of GR to abortion is similar—we need only switch from a blindness-drug (which blinds the fetus) to a death-drug (which kills the fetus). Your mother could have killed you through such a death-drug (or other means of abortion). Do you think this would have been all right—and do you consent to (or approve of) the idea of her having done this? Again the answer is a clear *no*—and an equally clear *no* regardless of the time of pregnancy that we imagine the killing taking place. We can argue as we did concerning blinding:

> If you are consistent and think that *abortion is normally permissible,* then you will consent to the idea of *your having been aborted* in normal circumstances. (From GR)
>
> You do not consent to the idea of your having been aborted in normal circumstances.
>
> Therefore, if you are consistent then you will not think that abortion is normally permissible.

Again with most people the second premise will be true—most people can be presumed not to consent to (or approve of) the idea of this act having been done to them. So insofar as most people take a consistent position they will not think that abortion is normally permissible.

IV. SIX OBJECTIONS

(1) Surely a utilitarian would see your two drug cases as very different—the blindness-drug inflicts needless future suffering while the death-drug simply eliminates a life. Why wouldn't a utilitarian, moved by the greatest total happiness principle, approve of the death-drug having been given to him if this would have led to a greater total happiness? Wouldn't such a person be a consistent upholder of the view that abortion is normally permissible?

My answer is that utilitarianism leads to so many strange moral implications that, even *if* the utilitarian could be consistent on this one case, still he would likely be inconsistent in his overall position. I previously claimed that utilitarianism would justify so many bizarre actions (including so many killings) that we would not accept this principle if we were consistent and realized its logical consequences. But if there are few (if any) consistent utilitarians then there would be few (if any) consistent utilitarian upholders of the view that abortion is normally permissible.

(2) Let us consider a *nonutilitarian* who approves of abortion but not infanticide or the blindness-drug. Why couldn't such a person consent to the idea of himself having been aborted under imagined or actual normal circumstances—and hence be consistent?

Such a person could be consistent, but only with bizarre desires about how he himself is to be treated. Let us suppose that someone combined these three judgments (as many are being brought up to do in our society today):

(a) It is wrong to blind an adult or child or infant or fetus.

(b) It is wrong to kill an adult or child or infant.

(c) It is permissible to kill a fetus.

To be consistent the person would have to answer these questions as follows:

Do you consent to the idea of my *blinding* you now?—NO!	Do you consent to the idea of my *killing* you now?—NO!
Do you consent to the idea of my having *blinded* you yesterday?—NO!	Do you consent to the idea of my having *killed* you yesterday?—NO!
. . . when you were five years old?—NO!	. . . when you were five years old?—NO!
. . . when you were one day old?—NO!	. . . when you were one day old?—NO!
. . . before you were born?—NO!	. . . before you were born?—*YES!!!*

It is strange that the person *disapproves equally* of being *blinded* at the various times—and *disapproves equally* of being *killed* at the first four times —and yet *approves* of being *killed* at the last time. He opposes the blindings because, regardless of their timing, the effect would be the same—he would be blind. He opposes the killings at the first four times because, again, the effect would be the same—he would not be alive; but killing at the fifth time has the same effect—why should he not oppose this killing also? The *yes* here seems rather strange. Of course one who thinks his life not worth living could give a *yes* to the idea of his having been killed while a fetus—but then we would expect *yes* answers to the idea of his being killed at the other times as well (which would make him inconsistent if he held that it is wrong to kill an adult or child or infant). So while a nonutilitarian who combines the three judgments above *could* in principle have such desires and be consistent, still this is unlikely to happen very often—to be consistent the person would have to have very bizarre desires.[6]

(3) Are you saying that the desires that most people have are good while unusual (or "bizarre") desires are bad? How would you establish this?

I am not saying that common desires are good while unusual desires are bad—often the reverse is true; and sometimes when we notice a conflict between our moral beliefs and our desires we come to change our desires and not our moral beliefs. Rather I am appealing to desires that most people have because I am trying to develop a consistency argument to show that most people who adopt the pro-abortion view are inconsistent. In effect I am challenging those who adopt such a view by saying, "Look at what you would have to desire in order to be consistent in your position—go and think about it and see whether you really are consistent!" I claim that most of the times the pro-abortionist will find that he is indeed inconsistent—he is supporting certain moral principles about the treatment of others that he would not wish to have been followed in their actions toward him.

(4) You question the consistency of one who holds that abortion is permissible but infanticide is wrong. But let us see whether you are consistent. If it would have been wrong for your parents to have aborted you, wouldn't it have been equally wrong for your parents not to have conceived you? The result would have been the same—there would be no YOU!

My answer here is complicated. My first reaction is to disapprove of the idea of my parents not having conceived me—to think it would have been wrong for them to have abstained or used contraceptives; but the universalizing requirement forces me to change my reactions (whereas it doesn't do this in the abortion case). If I hold "It is wrong to have an abortion in this (my) case," then I have to make the same judgment in all similar cases; but I can easily hold (consistently) that it is in general wrong to have an abortion. But if I hold "It is wrong to prevent conception (by, e.g., abstinence or contraceptives) in this (my) case," then I again have to make the same judgment in all similar cases; but I cannot hold (consistently) that it is in general wrong to prevent conception—since this would commit me to desiring a policy which would bring about a greatly overpopulated world of starving people at a very low level of human life. So, in order to be consistent, I change my first reaction and come to judge that it would have been morally permissible for my parents not to have conceived (me) on August 5, 1944—but instead perhaps to have conceived (someone else) on September 5, 1944—and I come, though with hesitation, to consent to the possibility of their having done this. To sum up: the universalizing requirement points to an important difference between *aborting* and *not conceiving*—I can "will as a universal law" a general prohibition against *aborting,* but not one against *nonconceiving.*

> (5) Suppose that reason does force us into thinking that abortion is *normally* wrong. What does "normal" here mean? And aren't the "abnormal" or "unusual" cases the more important and difficult ones to deal with? So isn't your conclusion unimportant?

My claim that abortion is *normally* wrong means that it is wrong in at least the great majority of cases but perhaps not in every conceivable case (e.g., in the imagined case where Dr. Evil will destroy the world if we do not do an abortion). The question of what unusual conditions (if any) would justify abortion is indeed important and difficult. But I think that, in light of the very great number of "convenience abortions" going on today, the issue of the general moral status of abortion is at the present time far more important.

> (6) Suppose that *if I am consistent* I cannot hold that abortion is normally permissible. What if I do not care about being consistent? Can you prove to me that I ought to care? Or can you prove to me that abortion is wrong without appealing to consistency?

You ask too much. Suppose I give you an argument proving that abortion is wrong (or that you ought to care about being consistent). If you do not already care about consistency, why should you not accept the premises of my argument and yet reject the conclusion? This would be inconsistent— but you don't care about this! So you presumably wouldn't care about any argument I might give—in effect you are saying that you have a closed mind. If you don't care about consistency then I am wasting my time when I try to reason with you.

NOTES

1. Tooley's original argument was in "Abortion and Infanticide," *Philosophy and Public Affairs* 2 (1972), pages 37–65. [See pp. 45–60 of the present volume.] He added refinements to his view in *Philosophy and Public Affairs* 2 (1973), pages 419–432; in a postscript to a reprint of his article in *The Rights and Wrongs of Abortion,* edited by Marshall Cohen, Thomas Nagel, and Thomas Scanlon (Princeton, 1974), pages 80–84; and in "In Defense of Abortion annd Infanticide," in *The Problem of Abortion* (second edition), edited by Joel Feinberg (Belmont, Calif., 1984), pages 120–134. (The weak link in the latest version of the argument seems to be this premise: 'An individual existing at one time cannot have desires at other

times unless there is at least one time at which it possesses the concept of a continuing self or mental substance'; this entails the incredible 'Your pet kitten cannot yesterday have had a desire to eat unless at some time it possesses the concept of a continuing self or mental substance.') Peter Singer's defense of abortion and infanticide rests partially on Tooley's earlier argument but mainly on his preference utilitarianism; see chapters 4 and 6 of his *Practical Ethics* (Cambridge, 1979).

2. Clause (f) was phrased to skirt the issue of Tooley's "superkittens" who become rational if given a certain drug; my intuitions on the superkitten (and Frankenstein) cases are not very clear. Clause (f) may require further refinement.

3. "A Defense of Abortion," in *Philosophy and Public Affairs* 1 (1971), pages 47–66. [See pp. 29–44 of the present volume.]

4. *The Right and the Good* (Oxford, 1930), page 19.

5. In arguing the abortion issue, I use some ideas from the theory of R. M. Hare, as developed in his *Freedom and Reason* (Oxford, 1963). Hare once wrote an article on "Abortion and the Golden Rule" (*Philosophy and Public Affairs* 4 (1975), pages 201-222); but his approach differs from mine. Hare rests his case on 'We should do to others what we are glad was done to us' and on the fact that we are glad that we were conceived, not aborted, and not killed as infants; hence we too ought to conceive, not abort, and not kill infants (but contraception, abortion, and infanticide turn out to have only a weak *prima facie* wrongness which is easy to override by other considerations). Hare's formulation of the golden rule here is defective; if I am *glad* my parents gave me hundreds of gifts each Christmas, then perhaps to be consistent I must hold that it would be good to do this same thing in similar circumstances—but I need not hold that one *should* do this (that it is a *duty*). Also my conclusions differ from Hare's—I view abortion and infanticide (but not failing-to-conceive) as seriously wrong; I think my conclusions are what Hare's theory should lead to.

6. On the Tooley/Singer view the cut-off point for killing is not birth but rather when the child comes to desire its continued existence as a continuing subject of experiences. (It is unclear at what age this happens.) My response to this view would be much like the above, except that the killing side of the chart would now have one more *yes*.

Concerning Abortion: An Attempt at a Rational View

Charles Hartshorne

My onetime colleague T. V. Smith once wrote a book called *Beyond Conscience,* in which he waxed eloquent in showing "the harm that good men do." To live according to one's conscience may be a fine thing, but what if *A*'s conscience leads *A* to try to compel *B* and *C* to live, not according to *B*'s or *C*'s conscience, but according to *A*'s? That is what many opponents of abortion are trying to do. To propose a constitutional amendment to this effect is one of the most outrageous attempts to tyrannize over others that I can recall in my long lifetime as an American citizen. Proponents of the anti-abortion amendment make their case, if possible, even worse when they defend themselves with the contention "It isn't my conscience only—it is a commandment of religion." For now one particular form of religion (certainly not the only form) is being used in an attempt to tyrannize over other forms of religious or philosophical belief. The separation of church and state evidently means little to such people.

IN WHAT SENSE "HUMAN"

Ours is a country that has many diverse religious groups, and many people who cannot find truth in any organized religious body. It is a country that has great difficulty in effectively opposing forms of killing that *everyone* admits to be wrong. Those who would saddle the legal system with matters about which consciences sincerely and strongly differ show a disregard of the country's primary needs. (The same is to be said about crusades to make things difficult for homosexuals.) There can be little freedom if we lose sight of the vital distinction between moral questions and legal ones. The law compels and coerces, with the implicit threat of violence; morals seek to persuade. It is a poor society that forgets this difference.

What is the *moral* question regarding abortion? We are told that the fetus is alive and that therefore killing it is wrong. Since mosquitoes, bacteria, apes and whales are also alive, the argument is less than clear. Even plants are alive. I am not impressed by the rebuttal "But plants, mosquitoes, bacteria and whales are not human, and the fetus is." For the issue now becomes, *in what sense* is the fetus human? No one denies that its origin is human, as is its *possible* destiny. But the same is true of every fertilized egg in the body of a nun. Is it wrong that some such eggs are not made or allowed to become human individuals?

Granted that a fetus is human in origin and possible destiny, in what further sense is it human? The entire problem lies here. If there are pro-life activists who have thrown much light on this question, I do not know their names.

One theologian who writes on the subject—Paul Ramsey—thinks that a human egg cell becomes a human individual with a moral claim to survive if it has been fertilized. Yet this egg cell has none of the qualities that we have in mind when we proclaim our superior worth to the chimpanzees or dolphins. It cannot speak, reason or judge between right and wrong. It cannot have personal relations, without which a person is not functionally a person at all, until months—and not, except minimally, until years—have passed. And even then, it will not be a person in the normal sense unless some who are already fully persons have taken pains to help it become a human being in the full value sense, functioning as such. The anti-abortionist is commanding some person or persons to undertake this effort. For without it, the fetus will *never* be human in the relevant sense. It will be human only in origin, but otherwise a subhuman animal.

The fertilized egg is an individual egg, but not an individual human being. For such a being is, in its body, a multicellular organism, a *metazoan*—to use the scientific Greek—and the egg is a single cell. The first thing the egg cell does is to begin dividing into many cells. For some weeks the fetus is not a single individual at all, but a colony of cells. During its first weeks there seems to be no ground for regarding the fetus as comparable to an individual animal. Only in possible or probable destiny is it an individual. Otherwise it is an organized society of single-celled individuals.

A possible individual person is one thing; an actual person is another. If this difference is not important, what is? There is in the long run no room in the solar system, or even in the known universe, for all human eggs—even all fertilized eggs, as things now stand—to become human persons. Indeed, it is mathematically demonstrable that the present rate of population growth must be lowered somehow. It is not a moral imperative that all possibilities of human persons become actual persons.

Of course, some may say that the fertilized egg already has a human soul, but on what evidence? The evidence of soul in the relevant sense is the capacity to reason, judge right and wrong, and the like.

GENETIC AND OTHER INFLUENCES

One may also say that since the fertilized egg has a combination of genes (the units of physical inheritance) from both parents, in this sense it is already a human individual. There are two objections, either one in my opinion conclusive but only one of which is taken into account by Ramsey. The one he does mention is that identical twins have the same gene combination. The theologian does not see this as decisive, but I do.

The other objection is that it amounts to a very crude form of materialism to identify individuality with the gene-combination. Genes are the chemical bearers of inherited traits. This chemical basis of inheritance presumably influences everything about the development of the individual—*influences*, but does not fully determine. To say that the entire life of the person is determined by heredity is a theory of unfreedom that my religious conviction can only regard as monstrous. And there are biophysicists and neurophysiologists who agree with me.

From the gene-determined chemistry to a human person is a long, long step. As soon as the nervous system forming in the embryo begins to function as a whole—and not before—the cell colony begins to turn into a genuinely individual animal. One may reasonably suppose that this change is accompanied by some extremely primitive individual animal feelings. They cannot be recognizably human feelings, much less human thoughts, and cannot compare with the feelings of a porpoise or chimpanzee in level of consciousness. That much seems as certain as anything about the fetus except its origin and possible destiny. The nervous system of a very premature baby has been compared by an expert to that of a pig. And we know, if we know anything about this matter, that it is the nervous system that counts where individuality is concerned.

Identical twins are different individuals, each unique in consciousness. Though having the same genetic makeup, they will have been differently situated in the womb and hence will have received different stimuli. For that reason, if for no other, they will have developed differently, especially in their brains and nervous systems.

But there are additional reasons for the difference in development. One is the role of chance, which takes many forms. We are passing through a great cultural change in which the idea, long dominant in science, that chance is "only a word for our ignorance of causes" is being replaced by the view that the real laws of nature are probabilistic and allow for aspects of genuine chance.

Another reason is that it is reasonable to admit a reverse influence of the developing life of feelings in the fetus on the nervous system, as well as of the system upon the feelings. And since I, along with some famous philosophers and scientists, believe in freedom (not solely of mature human beings but—in some slight degree—of all individuals in nature, down to the atoms and farther), I hold that even in the fetus the incipient individual is unconsciously making what on higher levels we call "decisions." These decisions influence the developing nervous system. Thus to a certain extent we *make our own bodies* by our feelings and thoughts. An English poet with Platonic ideas expressed this concept as follows:

> The body from the soul its form doth take,
> For soul is form and doth the body make.

The word soul is, for me, incidental. The point is that feelings, thoughts, experiences react on the body and partly mold its development.

THE RIGHTS OF PERSONS

Paul Ramsey argues (as does William Buckley in a letter to me) that if a fetus is not fully human, then neither is an infant. Of course an infant is not fully human. No one thinks it can, while an infant, be taught to speak, reason or judge right and wrong. But it is much closer to that stage than is a three-month fetus. It is beginning to have primitive social relations not open to a fetus; and since there is no sharp line anywhere between an infant and a child able to speak a few words, or between the latter and a child able to speak very many words, we have to regard the infant as significantly different from a three-month or four-month fetus. Nevertheless, I have little sympathy with the idea that infanticide is just another form of murder. Persons who are already functionally persons in the full sense have more important rights even than infants. Infanticide can be wrong without being fully comparable to the killing of persons in the full sense.

Does this distinction apply to the killing of a hopelessly senile person (or one in a permanent coma)? For me it does. I hope that no one will think that if, God forbid, I ever reach that stage, it must be for my sake that I should be treated with the respect due to normal human beings.

Rather, it is for the sake of others that such respect may be imperative. Symbolically, one who has been a person may have to be treated as a person. There are difficulties and hazards in not so treating such individuals.

Religious people (I would so describe myself) may argue that once a fetus starts to develop, it is for God, not human beings, to decide whether the fetus survives and how long it lives. This argument assumes, against all evidence, that human life-spans are independent of human decisions. Our medical hygiene has radically altered the original "balance of nature." Hence the population explosion. Our technology makes pregnancy more and more a matter of human decision; more and more our choices are influencing the weal and woe of the animals on this earth. It is an awesome responsibility, but one that we cannot avoid. And, after all, the book of Genesis essentially predicted our dominion over terrestrial life. In addition, no one is proposing to make abortion compulsory for those morally opposed to it. I add that everyone who smokes is taking a hand in deciding how long he or she will live. Also everyone who, by failing to exercise reasonably, allows his or her heart to lose its vigor. Our destinies are not simply "acts of God."

I may be told that if I value my life I must be glad that I was not aborted in the fetus state. Yes, I am glad, but this expression does not constitute a claim to having already had a "right," against which no other right could prevail, to the life I have enjoyed. I feel no indignation or horror at contemplating the idea the world might have had to do without me. The world could have managed, and as for what I would have missed, there would have been no such "I" to miss it.

POTENTIAL, NOT ACTUAL

With almost everything they say, the fanatics against abortion show that they will not, or cannot, face the known facts of this matter. The inability of a fetus to say "I" is not merely a lack of skill; there is nothing there to which the pronoun could properly refer. A fetus is not a person but a *potential* person. The "life" to which "pro-life" refers is nonpersonal, by any criterion that makes sense to some of us. It is subpersonal animal life only. The mother, however, *is* a person.

I resent strongly the way many males tend to dictate to females their behavior, even though many females encourage them in this. Of course, the male parent of a fetus also has certain rights, but it remains true that the female parent is the one most directly and vitally concerned.

I shall not forget talking about this whole matter to a wonderful woman, the widow of a philosopher known for his idealism. She was doing social work with young women and had come to the conclusion that abortion is, in some cases, the lesser evil. She told me that her late husband had said, when she broached the subject to him, "But you can't do that." "My darling," she replied, "we *are* doing it." I see no reason to rate the consciences of the pro-lifers higher than this woman's conscience. She knew what the problem was for certain mothers. In a society that flaunts sex (its pleasures more than its serious hazards, problems, and spiritual values) in all the media, makes it difficult for the young to avoid unwanted pregnancy, and does little to help them with the most difficult of all problems of self-discipline, we tell young persons that they are murderers if they resort to abortion. And so we should not be surprised that Margaret Mead, the clear-sighted observer of our society (and of other societies), should say, "Abortion is a nasty thing, but our society deserves it." Alas, it is too true.

I share something of the disgust of hard-core opponents of abortion that contraceptives, combined with the availability of abortion, may deprive sexual intercourse of spiritual meaning. For me the sacramental view of marriage has always had appeal, and my life has been lived accordingly. Abortion is indeed a nasty thing, but unfortunately there are in our society many even nastier things, like the fact that some children are growing up unwanted. This for my conscience is a great deal nastier, and truly horrible. An overcrowded world is also nasty, and could in a few decades become truly catastrophic.

The argument against abortion (used, I am sorry to say, by Pearl Buck) that the fetus may be a potential genius has to be balanced against the much more probable chance of its being a mediocrity, or a destructive enemy of society. Every egg cell is a possible genius and also a possible monster in human form. Where do we stop in calculating such possibilities?

If some who object to abortion work to diminish the number of unwanted, inappropriate pregnancies, or to make bearing a child for adoption by persons able to be its loving foster parents more attractive than it now is, and do this with a minimum of coercion, all honor to them. In view of the population problem, the first of these remedies should have high priority.

Above all, the coercive power of our legal system, already stretched thin, must be used with caution and chiefly against evils about which there is something like universal consensus. That persons have rights is a universal belief in our society, but that a fetus is already an actual person—about that there is and there can be no consensus. Coercion in such matters is tyranny. Alas for our dangerously fragmented and alienated society if we persist in such tyranny.

The Fetus and Fundamental Rights

Joan C. Callahan

THE CONSISTENCY PROBLEM

Although the 1984 presidential election is history, the campaigns raised a number of questions which have not been resolved, and which need more public discussion. Not the least among these are the questions that surrounded Geraldine Ferraro's position on abortion—a position that significantly disrupted her campaign, and which, during the early fall of 1984, put all liberal Democratic Catholic politicians into political trouble from which they have not yet escaped.[1]

The trouble was focused on the question of abortion, but the problem is deeper than any single issue. The problem is one of consistency: How can a politician believe that something is profoundly morally wrong, yet insist that he or she will not use political power to right the wrong? The reply from the Geraldine Ferraros and Edward Kennedys was that it is not the proper business of the politician to impose his or her religious beliefs on members of a pluralistic society. Although this is surely true, it was an inadequate response. It was inadequate because it missed the point; and it missed the point because it seemed to treat matters like our public policy on abortion as if they were the same in kind as eating meat on Friday or making one's Easter Duty. The Catholic politicians may not have been making a category mistake, but they certainly sometimes sounded as if they were. Bishop James Timlin of Scranton did not have to be a bishop, a Roman Catholic, or even a Christian to say with understandable astonishment that Geraldine Ferraro's position on abortion is like saying "I'm

This is a revised version of an article that appeared in *Commonweal* (April 11, 1986):203-209. Reprinted by permission of the author and the publisher.

personally opposed to slavery, but I don't care if people down the street want to own slaves."[2] The Catholic liberal Democrats thought and think this analogy fails. But *why* it fails was never made clear. In what follows, I want to address Bishop Timlin's analogy and hence, the particular question of abortion, as well as the larger question of appropriate reasons for a politician's policy choices. My purpose is to get clearer on both the morality of elective abortion and the question of moral consistency in political life.

RELIGIOUS V. PHILOSOPHICAL REASONS

Bishop Timlin's analogy is faulty in at least three ways. First, refusing to use the law to fight a practice one believes is immoral does not imply that one does not *care* if people engage in that practice. Mario Cuomo, in his thoughtful, if not wholly adequate, speech at Notre Dame made that very clear.[3] There is no doubt that Mr. Cuomo cares deeply about abortion. But we can cite any number of examples (e.g., the selfish breaking of promises, the telling of lies to friends for bad reasons, etc.) of actions we believe are morally wrong and about which we care, but which we do not (and should not) attempt to eradicate by law. Thus, it does not follow from the fact that someone is unwilling to pursue a legal prohibition on some kind of activity that the person does not care if people engage in that activity. Nor does it follow from the fact that one believes that some kind of action is morally wrong that one is morally obligated to seek a legal prohibition on that kind of action.

Bishop Timlin's analogy is also faulty because it fails to recognize that the *reasons* one has for holding something to be wrong are of the utmost importance when one is trying to decide whether to pursue a legal prohibition on individual liberty. In a pluralistic society, the fact that a religious institution, or a religious contingency (no matter how large), holds something to be wrong is simply not a good reason for setting a public policy prohibiting or requiring action on the part of all citizens. Insofar as a Catholic politician's reason for holding that abortion is wrong is that this is church doctrine, there can be no obligation to try to institute a prohibition on abortion on those who do not share the same religious affiliation. Indeed, part of the politician's obligation in a pluralistic society is to guard against just such impositions by religious groups. In the vice-presidential debate, Congresswoman Ferraro made it clear that her reason for being "personally" opposed to abortion is that her church holds this as doctrine. If this is indeed *why* she is opposed to abortion, then it ought to be clear to all of us that she has no more duty (or right) to try to capture her opposition to abortion in law than she has to try to force Americans who do not share her religious affiliation to attend Roman Catholic Mass weekly. And the same is true for any other politician who is opposed to abortion *because* this is a doctrine of his or her faith.[4]

   But there are other reasons for being opposed to abortion—philosophical reasons which appeal to the laws of logic and to moral rights—which might be shared by the most ardent atheist. Many who are opposed to abortion have these kinds of reasons for holding that abortion is wrong, and so profoundly wrong that it might be rightly prohibited by law, even in a pluralistic society. We need, then, to make a distinction between those who hold that abortion is wrong simply because their religion says so, and those who think that abortion is wrong because they believe that the philosophical reasons compel us to accept that human fetuses have a right which is comparable to your right and my right not to be killed.

   Reasons of the first kind (i.e., purely religious reasons) are excellent reasons for acting or not acting in certain ways in one's own life, but they are bad reasons for imposing legal requirements or legal restraints on those who do not share the same religious commitments. We all know this. If some new, large religious contingency were to come to believe that zero population growth is the will of God, and if the government set out to capture this belief in law, Roman Catholics and other Christians would lead the ranks of civil disobedients. But reasons of the second kind (i.e., reasons appealing to the logic of human rights) are of the appropriate kind to justify or even require someone's working for legal prohibitions on certain actions or practices. The problem in the abortion debate is that there is a profound disagreement about the relative strengths of the philosophical reasons given for and against holding that elective abortion is the killing of an unconsenting innocent person for inadequate moral reasons. If an elective abortion *is* the killing of an unconsenting innocent person for reasons which would not justify killing an adult person, then it is wrongful killing, and a policy allowing elective abortion cannot be morally justified. But *are* human fetuses persons? The question is a sensible one, and there are responsible philosophical reasons for saying yes and there are responsible philosophical reasons for saying no. And that's the rub.

FETAL RIGHTS AND THE LOGICAL WEDGE

Those who oppose elective abortion often insist that human life begins at conception. But this is just wrong. Human life begins long before conception. The sperm and egg are alive, and they are not bovine or feline or canine— they are living human gametes. To couch the question in terms of the beginning of human life is to muddle the issue. It is to make the question of the morality of abortion sound like one that can be answered by a very cleaver biologist. But the issue is not when human life begins. Unquestionably, human fetuses are, from the earliest stages, alive. What we *really* want to know is whether the living human fetus should be recognized as a bearer of the same range of fundamental moral rights that you and I have, among them the right not to be killed without *very* good reason. And the most clever biologist in the world cannot answer this for us, since the question is simply not a biological one.

But it might be objected that although some who are opposed to abortion and who have not thought carefully enough about the issue do made the mistake of thinking that the question is when biological life begins, it is also true that not everyone who talks in terms of the beginning of human life is making this mistake. For surely many who are opposed to elective abortion mean to contend that the life of a *unique* human being, of a distinct *person,* begins at conception, and that is why a policy allowing abortion is wrong.

The problem with this response, however, is that it is not a single claim. For one can grant that the life of a unique human being begins at conception, yet not grant that a distinct person emerges at conception, since the two claims are not equivalent unless one begs the question in favor of fetal personhood. That is, if we mean by "human being" "a member of the biological species, *Homo sapiens,*" then (if we ignore the problem of identical twins) it is uncontroversially true that the life of a unique human being begins at conception. This is merely a scientific claim, and it is one that can be conclusively defended by scientists as such. But the claim that a distinct *person* emerges at conception is not a scientific one; for to call something "a person" is already to assert that it is a bearer of strongest moral rights—fundamental rights comparable to yours and mine, among them the right not to be killed except for the most compelling of moral reasons. If in asserting that "a human life begins at conception" the opponent of elective abortion means to assert the biological claim, that can be granted immediately. But if he or she means to assert that "a person emerges at conception," that is a very different claim—it is a moral claim. Indeed, it is the very claim that is at issue in the abortion debate. What those who oppose retaining a policy of elective abortion need to tell us is *why* we must accept that the truth of the biological claim commits us to accepting the moral claim.

But those opposed to elective abortion might still respond that those who admit that the life of a unique human being (in the biological sense) begins at conception are indeed committed to granting that (insofar as human fetuses become distinct persons) the life of a distinct person begins here as well. For where did the life of any adult person begin but at conception?

There are, however, at least two responses to this. The first is simply to make the logical point that one can allow that the life of a person begins at conception without allowing that the (biological human) being present at conception is yet a person. That is, just as one can allow that the first tiny bud in an acorn is the beginning of the life of a (future) oak tree without being committed to saying that the bud is already an oak tree, one can allow that conception marks the beginning of the life of a (future) person without being committed to saying that the conceptus is already a person.

This logical point leads to the second, more substantive, response: namely, that we think the tiny bud in the acorn is quite clearly *not* an oak tree. And we think this because the bud does not yet have the characteristics of oak trees. Indeed, acorns with tiny buds are very *unlike* oak trees, even though every oak tree began as a bud in an acorn. In just the same way, the new conceptus is very unlike beings who have the kinds of characteristics which compel us to recognize them as persons. What kinds of characteristics are these? I cannot offer a full account here, but perhaps it will be enough to point out that if we came across a being like [the motion picture character] E.T. (who is not biologically human), we would surely think him a person— a being with fundamental moral rights comparable to yours and mine. And this would be because we would recognize that he has certain characteristics— the capacity to suffer mental and physical pain, the ability to make plans, a sense of himself as an ongoing being, and so on—which are sufficient to compel us to hold that he must (and must not) be treated in certain ways. (And, of course, the film, *E.T.*, turns on precisely this point.) A conceptus, however, has none of these characteristics. Indeed, like the mystery of the acorn and the oak, what is amazing is that such radically *different* beings emerge from such beginnings. But it needs to be clearly recognized that in the case of the acorn and in the case of the conceptus, at the end of the process, we do have beings *very* unlike those at the beginning of the process.[3]

When, then, must we say of a developing human being that we must recognize it as a person? If we are talking about when we have a being with the kinds of characteristics we take to be relevant to compelling a recognition of human personhood, it seems that persons (at least human persons) are, like oak trees, emergent beings, and that deciding when to classify a developing human being as a person is like deciding when to call a shoot a tree. Young trees do not have all the characteristics of grown trees—for example, children cannot safely swing from them. But when a shoot begins to take on at least some of the characteristics of full-fledged trees, we think we are not confused in beginning to call that shoot a tree. Similarly, there is no clear distinction between where the Mississippi River ends and the Gulf of Mexico begins. But settle the issue by setting a *convention* which does not seem counterintuitive. We are faced with quite the same kind of question when it comes to the matter of persons. Since fetuses do not have the kinds of characteristics which compel us to recognize beings as persons, we must, whether we like it or not, sit down and *decide* whether fetuses are to be recognized as full-fledged persons as a matter of public policy.

And we must decide the question on the basis of the appropriate kinds of reasons. That is, for the purposes of setting public policy in a religiously heterogeneous society, we must decide it on the basis of the nonreligious, philosophical arguments, some of which urge us to accept that we must recognize human fetuses as having the same range of fundamental rights that you and I have, and some of which hold that this is just not so.

One possible convention is to set the recognition of personhood at birth. Still others might be at various stages of prenatality or at various points after birth. Those who oppose elective abortion insist that we *must* recognize personhood at conception, and central to the position is most frequently an argument known as "the logical wedge." This argument holds that if we are going to recognize older children as having the same fundamental rights that you and I have, then logic compels us to recognize that, from the moment of conception, all human beings must have those same rights. The argument proceeds by starting with beings everyone recognizes as having the rights in question and then by pointing out that a child (say) at fifteen is not radically different from one at fourteen and a half; and a child at fourteen and a half is not radically different from one at fourteen, and so on. The argument presses us back from fourteen to thirteen to twelve—to infancy. From infancy, it is a short step to late-term fetuses, because (the argument goes) change in location (from the womb to the wider world) does not constitute an essential change in the being itself. *You* do not lose *your* right not to be killed simply by walking from one room to another. Similarly, it is argued, mere change of place is not philosophically important enough to justify such a radical difference in treatment between infants and late-term fetuses. The argument then presses us back to early-term fetuses—back to conception. Logic and fairness, then, force us to accept that even the new conceptus has the same fundamental right to life that you and I have.

But those who support retaining a policy of elective abortion often point out that this kind of argument for fetal rights is faulty, since if we accept that we can never treat beings who are not radically different from one another in radically different ways, we shall be unable to justify all sorts of public policies which we want to keep and which we all believe are fair. It is argued, for example, that this kind of argument for fetal rights entails that we cannot be justified in setting driving or voting ages, since withholding these privileges until a certain age discriminates against those close to that age: An eighteen-year-old is not radically different from a seventeen-and-a-half-year-old, and so on. Thus, the implication of this kind of argument is that setting ages for the commencement of certain important societal privileges cannot be morally justified. We must give the five-year-old the right to vote, the six-year-old the right to drink, the nine-year-old the right to drive. But these implications, it is argued, show that this kind of argument for fetal rights is unsound.[6]

The response to this criticism of the logical wedge argument, however, is that the granting of societal privileges is not a matter of arbitrariness, even if there is some arbitrariness in selecting ages for the commencement of such privileges. Proper use of these rights, it may be argued, requires a cerain degree of maturity—responsibility, background knowledge, experience, independence, and, in the case of driving, a certain degree of developed physical dexterity. Thus, it is because certain changes normally occur as a child matures into an adult that it is appropriate to set policies which acknowledge those changes. But this, it may be argued, is not the case when it comes to recognizing the right to life. That is, those who oppose retaining a policy of elective abortion insist that after conception *no* changes occur that are relevant to recognizing the personhood (and thus the right to life) of a human being.

But this immediately takes us back to the acorn and the oak. The bud and the tree simply *are* significantly different kinds of beings. And you and I *are* significantly different from a conceptus, which has *none* of the characteristics which morally compel us to recognize it as a being with rights. It will not do simply to deny that there are significant changes between the time of conception and the time when we have a being which we simply *must* recognize as a bearer of rights. Thus, we are once again confronted with the question of deciding where we shall set the convention of recognizing personhood.

At this point, however, there is yet another response open to the opponent of elective abortion—namely, that the kind of reasoning used to defeat the argument for fetal rights cannot be correct, since it will not only rule out our being committed to the rights of fetuses, it also entails that we are not compelled to accept that human infants are beings of a kind which must be recognized as having the full range of fundamental moral rights, since infants are, it might be suggested, more like very young kittens in regard to the characteristics in question than they are like paradigm cases of persons.

But this objection is not devastating. For, again, the question before us is a question of deciding what convention we shall adopt. And one can allow that even if infants do not (yet) have the characteristics which compel us to accept a being as a person, there are other considerations which provide excellent reasons for taking birth as the best place to set the convention of recognizing personhood and the full range of fundamental moral rights, despite the fact that infants as such are far more like very young kittens than they are like beings whose characteristics compel us to accept them as full members of the moral community.

Chief among these considerations are the facts that persons other than an infant's biological mother are able to care for the infant and have an interest in doing so. There is no radical change in the characteristics of a human being just before birth and just after birth. But once a human being emerges from the womb and others are able to care for it, there are radical changes in what is involved in preserving its life. And the crucial change is that sustaining its life violates no right of its biological mother. Thus birth, which marks this change, is not an arbitrary point for commencing recognition of personhood.

It is important to notice here that to hold that a woman has a right to terminate a pregnancy is not to hold that she also has a right to the death of her fetus if that fetus can survive, and quite the same reasons that can justify a proscription on infanticide can justify a requirement to sustain viable fetuses that survive abortion. What we are not entitled to do, it may be argued, is force a woman to complete a pregnancy because others have an interest in having her fetus. But it does not follow from this that a woman may kill a born infant that can be cared for by others. Thus, it does not follow from the kind of reasoning I have sketched above that the defender of a policy allowing elective abortion is committed to a policy allowing infanticide. Indeed, the position is fully consistent with holding that even though infants do not yet possess the kinds of characteristics which compel recognition of a being as a person, the fact that they are now biologically independent beings that can be sustained without forcing an unwilling woman to serve as a life support provides an excellent reason for setting the convention of a right to life at birth, that is, viable emergence.[7]

Perhaps it should be pointed out here that the view I have just sketched can also allow that even kittens have *some* moral rights. I, for one, believe that as sentient beings—beings capable of suffering pain—they have a strong moral right not to be treated cruelly, that is, not to have pain wantonly imposed on them. Insofar as fetuses can suffer pain, the defender of elective abortion must be justified. To say this, however, is not to be committed to holding that fetuses must be recognized as having the same full range of fundamental rights that you and I have. It is, rather, to allow fetuses (at the very least) the moral standing of any being of comparable sentience, and, hence, to hold that there is always a moral obligation not to wantonly impose pain on fetuses. But given the exquisite intimacy of pregnancy, any woman who does not want to bring a child to term has a strong reason for seeking an abortion. Thus, if pain is imposed on the fetus in abortion, it is not wantonly imposed.[8]

But it will surely still be objected that human fetuses and human infants are beings that are potentially like paradigm cases of persons, and this makes them very *unlike* other beings of comparable sentience. Kittens, after all, will never develop the kinds of characteristics that compel us to recognize them as full-fledged members of the moral community, and because of this, we must recognize human fetuses as having a far more significant moral standing than other beings of comparable sentience. Sometimes opponents of elective abortion point this out, saying that from the moment of conception a fetus is a *potential* person, and must, therefore, be granted the right to life. But the problem here is that to say that a being is a potential person is just to say it is a person-not-yet, which is, of course, to deny that it is now a person. And this is to give the defender of the retaining choice in this area the very point that is crucial to his or her argument against the argument for fetal rights, and to thereby turn the question back to the question of deciding on a convention.

ACTUAL AND POTENTIAL PERSONS

The crucial question, then, is whether we should recognize the fetus as a person now or whether we should recognize the fetus as a potential person—as a person-not-yet. If we take the first choice, then the full range of fundamental moral rights attaches to the fetus. If we take the second choice, it remains an open question what moral duties we might have toward the fetus. Either way, our *reasons* for deciding as we do must be more than religious ones if the purpose of deciding is to set policy in a pluralistic society. Bishop Timlin's analogy to slavery fails yet a third time because there are no such open questions about involuntary slavery. Enslaving a person against his or her will is a paradigm case of injustice. But we haven't anything like the same sort of moral certainty about the injustice of abortion. And since we haven't, those who recognize the complexity of the question can hold, without being heartless or inconsistent, that *they* believe abortion is wrong, but also that they are unprepared to impose that view on those who remain reflectively unconvinced by the arguments that the human fetus must be recognized as having the full moral status of a person.

Does it follow from all this that there is some serious doubt about the personhood of fetuses—that is, that the fetus might be a person? Sometimes those who support retaining a policy of elective abortion say things like this—that the fetus *might* be a person, but that the evidence is just not conclusive. But if this is the position one holds, those who oppose allowing elective abortion have a strong response. That response is that we should give the fetus the benefit of the doubt. After all, if a hunter hears a movement in the bushes and shoots without making sure she is not shooting a person, and it turns out that she has killed or injured a person, we charge her with gross recklessness. And her saying that it was possible that what she shot at was not a person is no defense. She simply should not have shot if there were even a remote possibility that she would injure a person. In just the same way, the opponent of allowing elective abortion argues that if there is *any* possibility that the fetus is a person, we have a duty to act as if it were a person—a duty to avoid acting recklessly. And part of what *that* means is that another person may not kill it for reasons less than self-defense.

This is an interesting argument, but it misses an important point. For the real doubt is not whether a fetus is a person. Rather, if there is a doubt it is about whether we should treat something which is obviously a potential person (in the sense that it has potentially the characteristics of paradigm cases of persons) as if it were a person already. And this is not something that can be decided by going and looking at the fetus, as one might go and look in the bushes. For (again) in looking, we shall find that although fetuses are quite wonderful beings, they lack the kinds of characteristics that morally compel us to accept a being as a person. The question to be resolved, then, is whether we should accept that these beings which will emerge as persons if their lives are supported ought, at this stage of their development, be treated as if were persons already—as beings with a moral right to life comparable to yours and mine, comparably protected by the coercive power of the law.

When we are trying to resolve the real doubt, a large part of what we need to ask is what deciding to treat fetuses as beings with the full range of fundamental moral rights would really involve in practice, and whether our shared moral views about paradigm cases of persons will allow us to accept these things. Let us, then, look for a moment at just two of the implications of deciding to admit human fetuses into the class of full-fledged persons with full-fledged fundamental rights.

SOME IMPLICATIONS OF RECOGNIZING FETUSES AS PERSONS

If we decide to recognize fetuses as full persons, the first thing that follows (as Mr. Reagan has recognized) is that abortion in cases of rape or incest must be ruled out. Suppose that I were to discover that you are the product of rape or incest. You would not think (and none of us would think) that it followed from this that I could kill you. Fundamental rights are not a consequence of where someone came from. If we allow that human fetuses are persons, we could not consistently allow abortion for (say) an eighteen-year-old woman who had been raped by her father. What is more, if this woman were to perform an abortion on herself and be found out, we must treat her as we treat any murderer. In some jurisdictions, this might lead to life imprisonment or even execution. During the 1984 campaigns, President Reagan was asked in the first debate with Mr. Mondale whether he believed we should treat women who abort for reasons less than self-defense as murderers, with all that might entail. He avoided the question, saying that this would be a matter for the states to decide. But the opponent of elective abortion needs to confront this question squarely and honestly. Precisely what *are* we to do with women who abort? Can we accept that states may decide to imprison them or execute them? Just what are we to do with them? If the proponent of a probition on elective abortion confronts this question earnestly and *cannot* comfortably hold that jurisdictions *should* treat these women as they typically treat murderers, then he or she needs to begin to think carefully about *why.* When asked in the first debate to explain his position on abortion, Mr. Mondale (echoing Governor Cuomo) said of the prohibitive policy espoused by Mr. Reagan, "It won't work." This is a woefully inadequate response. But I suspect that what Mr. Mondale had in mind was that accepting the fetus as a full-fledged person commits us to measures in practice that even those who are deeply opposed to elective abortion cannot fully accept, among them that the eighteen-year-old who aborts a fetus resulting from rape by her father is to be treated as any murderer of a helpless, innocent person. We are not, even in this pluralistic society, free to kill others for reasons less than the immediate defense of our own lives, and if we do, we are subject to the most severe legal penalties, including possible execution. If fetuses are to be recognized as full-fledged persons, then justice requires that those who abort them for reasons less than self-defense must be recognized as full-fledged murderers and treated as such. Those who are rigorously opposed to retaining a policy of elective abortion on the ground that fetuses are persons must confront this implication sincerely and sensitively, and they must be explicit on what they are willing to accept as the practical implications of their position. If they are not willing to accept that those who abort should be subject to the exactly the same treatments as others who murder innocent persons, then they do not *really* believe that the fetus has precisely the same moral status as you and I.

There is yet another potent implication of recognizing fetuses as full-fledged persons. Mr. Reagan and Mr. Bush would both allow abortion in cases of self-defense—that is, in cases where the woman's life is threatened. But there is a problem with this position that generally goes unnoticed. For if our public policy is to recognize that the fetus is genuinely an innocent person, then its threat to a woman's life is an innocent threat, and the state can have no legitimate reason for systematically preferring the life of the woman to the life of the fetus.[9] That is, the argument from self-defense simply cannot justify the state's allowing a woman the use of medical specialists who will systematically prefer her life to the life of the fetus. If the fetus is a person who has precisely the same moral status as the woman, the state must, as a matter of fairness to the fetus, do nothing that would involve it in giving the woman an unfair advantage over the fetus. And, again, this means that the state should not permit the use of technologically advanced institutions or the use of technologically advanced practitioners which give the woman an unfair advantage in this battle for life between moral equals.

The argument from self-defense, then, seems to entail far greater restrictions on abortion than even the most fervent opponents of elective abortion tend to want to allow, Mr. Reagan among them. If opponents of elective abortion want to allow abortions in cases where the woman's life is at stake, then they must realize that implicit in their position is the view that the woman and the fetus are *not* of equal moral stature after all.

MORAL SENSITIVITY AND SETTING PUBLIC POLICY

My own view is that there are insurmountable difficulties to finding an argument for the recognition of fetuses as persons which is cogent and compelling enough to justify imposing on women the exquisitely intimate burden of bearing an unwanted child. But even if this view is correct, it does not follow that we can do just anything to human fetuses. Kittens are not persons, but we are not at moral liberty to wantonly impose pain on them. Natural resources are not persons, but we are not at moral liberty to wantonly destroy them. Several years ago, Patrick Buchanan wrote of an experiment on human fetuses, discussed in *The Second American Revolution*, by John Whitehead. Six months after *Roe* v. *Wade*, Dr. A. J. Adam of Case Western Reserve University reported to the American Pediatric Research Society that he and his associates had conducted an experiment on twelve fetuses, up to twenty weeks old, delivered alive by hysterectomy abortion. Adam and his associates cut the heads off these fetuses and cannulated the internal carotid arteries. They kept the heads alive, much as the Russians kept dogs' heads alive during the 1950s. When challenged, Dr. Adam's response was that society had decided that these fetuses would die, thus they had no rights. Said Adam, "I don't see any ethical problem." I find Dr. Adam's failure to see any ethical problem chilling and morally repugnant, even though these fetuses had no real chance of long-term survival *ex utero*. One of the legitimate worries of those who are opposed to abortion is that this kind of ghoulish insensitivity will become more and more prevalent in our society, spilling over to a cavalier attitude toward human life in general. One need not be absolutely opposed to allowing elective abortion to share that worry, and one need not think nonviable fetuses are persons to be astonished at Dr. Adam's failure to see *any* ethical problem.

When asked in the 1984 campaign debate about his position on abortion, Vice President Bush replied that he had changed his view (which previously had been more liberal) because of the number of legal abortions that have taken place in this country. But the problem with this reason for disallowing elective abortion is that it misses the very point of those who have traditionally opposed abortion; for if fetuses have the same range of moral rights that you and I have, then even one abortion for reasons less than those which would justify killing an adult person is too many. Determining moral rights is not a numbers game. We don't have laws against murder because there are too many murders—we have laws against murder because every single person has a compelling moral right not to be murdered. Because that right is so compelling, the state comes forward to protect it. When one understands that persons have a compelling moral right not to be murdered, one also understands that numbers of murders are irrelevant to the question of whether society should have laws against murder. One murder is simply one too many. Mr. Bush's position, then, misses the very strong position on fundamental fetal rights that has been the moral centerpiece of the movement against elective abortion.

Still, there is much to be said for Mr. Bush's discomfort with the use of abortion as a form of birth control. Although I believe that defenders of retaining a policy of elective abortion who have thought carefully and sensitively about the issue are more than willing to admit that abortion, however well-justified, is never a happy moral choice, some who favor elective abortion angrily talk about fetuses as being, like tumors, morally equivalent to parasites. Such talk is inexcusably cavalier; and those who believe that the human fetus is of significant moral worth are understandably infuriated when they hear it or read it. Language like that does not help get us to reasonable, sensitive discussion. And it is precisely reasonable, sensitive discussion that we now most need on this difficult question of morality and public policy.

It should go without saying that public policy should not be set by those who shout the loudest—that it should not be set by those who carry the most emotively charged posters, or by those who use the most emotively charged language. But neither should it be carelessly set by an unreflective commitment to a woman's right to self-direction which fails to take into serious account the genuine moral costs of giving absolute priority to such a right. Public policy must be set by sitting down and coming to understand the legitimate concerns on both sides of hard issues. It must be set with an eye toward what *all* morally sensitive persons in a pluralistic society can live with.

The abortion issue is one about which reasonable people can disagree. We all need to realize this, and we need to do more talking instead of shouting. Deliberation in the philosophy of moral rights involves much more than repeating bumper sticker slogans; and rational agreement in such deliberation is often hard-won, and will only succeed when each side can see clearly why the other side begins from the position it does. It will not do, then, for those who are opposed to retaining a policy of elective abortion to call themselves "pro-life" and to call fetuses "babies" and take the issue to be settled. And it will not do for those who believe we must retain abortion as an option for women to call fetuses "parasites" and take the issue to be settled. Trying to decide public policy must involve refusing to use language which implies that the opposition is against something that any morally reasonable person would support or which simply begs the question against the other side. It must involve sensitive deliberation which takes carefully into account the deeply felt and morally reasonable concerns of a variety of perspectives. And the effort must lead to decisions that thoughtful persons in a pluralistic society can respect, no matter what policies they would prefer to see. Defenders and opponents of a policy of elective abortion must realize that we share a large common moral ground. We must begin to work from that common ground to come to an agreement on policies that can respectfully govern us all.

The liberal Catholic politicians are in trouble, and they will stay in trouble until they more adequately explain their reasons for not seeking a moratorium on elective abortion. Mario Cuomo began that explanation at Notre Dame. But there is much more to be said if all morally concerned Americans are to understand why politicians like Geraldine Ferraro and Mario Cuomo are neither necessarily inconsistent, nor rabid moral relativists, nor insensitive moral thugs.

NOTES

1. An edited version of this essay appeared in *Commonweal* 11 (April 1986) 203-9. I am deeply indebted to Peter Steinfels for his extensive and enormously helpful comments and questions on an earlier draft. For an expanded discussion of fetal rights, see James W. Knight and Joan C. Callahan, *Preventing Birth: Contemporary Methods and Related Moral Controversies* (Salt Lake City: University of Utah Press, 1989), chaps. 7 and 9.

2. *Newsweek,* Sept. 24, 1984.

3. Governor Cuomo's speech was given on Sept. 13, 1984.

4. I offer a more detailed account of what it means to be "personally" opposed to some kind of action in "Religion and Moral Consistency in Politics," in progress.

5. For a fuller discussion of the kinds of characteristics morally relevant to compelling a recognition of beings (including nonhuman beings) as persons see, e.g., Mary Anne Warren, "On the Moral and Legal Status of Abortion," in *Today's Moral Problems,* ed. Richard Wasserstrom (New York: Macmillan, 1975) 120-36 [see pages 75-82 of the present volume]. See also Jane English, "Abortion and the Concept of a Person," *Canadian Journal of Philosophy* 5, no. 2 (1975) 233-43 [see pages 83-94 of the present volume], for an even more detailed discussion of the cluster of features that enter into our concept of a person.

6. For a more detailed treatment of this response to the logical wedge, see, e.g., Jonathan Glover, *Causing Death and Saving Lives* (New York: Penguin, 1977), chap. 12.

7. Again, see Warren for a version of this line of reasoning.

8. I deal with this question of fetal sentience (as well as several related issues)

in more detail in "*The Silent Scream:* A New, Conclusive Argument Against Abortion?" *Philosophy Research Archives* 11 (1986): 181-95. On the question of fetal sentience, see also L. W. Sumner, *Abortion and Moral Theory* (Princeton: Princeton University Press, 1981), chap. 4. A revised version of that chapter appears as "A Third Way," in *The Problem of Abortion,* ed. Joel Feinberg, 2nd ed. (Belmont, Calif.: Wadsworth, 1984), pp. 71-93.

9. This point is argued in detail by Nancy Davis in "Abortion and Self-Defense," *Philosophy and Public Affairs* 13, no. 3 (Summer 1984): 175-207.

Abortion and the Sexual Agenda

Sidney Callahan

The abortion debate continues. In the latest and perhaps most crucial development, pro-life feminists are contesting pro-choice feminist claims that abortion rights are prerequisites for women's full development and social equality. The outcome of this debate may be decisive for the culture as a whole. Pro-life feminists, like myself, argue on good feminist principles that women can never achieve the fulfillment of feminist goals in a society permissive toward abortion.

These new arguments over abortion take place within liberal political circles. This round of intense intra-feminist conflict has spiraled beyond earlier right-versus-left abortion debates, which focused on "tragic choices," medical judgments, and legal compromises. Feminist theorists of the pro-choice position now put forth the demand for unrestricted abortion rights as a *moral imperative* and insist upon women's right to complete reproductive freedom. They morally justify the present situation and current abortion practices. Thus it is all the more important that pro-life feminists articulate their different feminist perspective. . . .

Pro-life feminists grant the good intentions of their pro-choice counterparts but protest that the pro-choice position is flawed, morally inadequate, and inconsistent with feminism's basic demands for justice. Pro-life feminists champion a more encompassing moral ideal. They recognize the claims of fetal life and offer a different perspective on what is good for women. The feminist vision is expanded and refocused.

From *Commonweal* (25 April 1986): 232-238. Reprinted by permission of the publisher.

FROM THE MORAL RIGHT TO CONTROL ONE'S OWN BODY
TO A MORE INCLUSIVE IDEAL OF JUSTICE

The moral right to control one's own body does apply to cases of organ transplants, mastectomies, contraception, and sterilization; but it is not a conceptualization adequate for abortion. The abortion dilemma is caused by the fact that 266 days following a conception in one body, another body will emerge. One's own body no longer exists as a single unit but is engendering another organism's life. This dynamic passage from conception to birth is genetically ordered and universally found in the human species. Pregnancy is not like the growth of cancer or infestation by a biological parasite; it is the way every human being enters the world. Strained philosophical analogies fail to apply: having a baby is not like rescuing a drowning person, being hooked up to a famous violinist's artificial life-support system, donating organs for transplant—or anything else.

As embryology and fetology advance, it becomes clear that human development is a continuum. Just as astronomers are studying the first three minutes in the genesis of the universe, so the first moments, days, and weeks at the beginning of human life are the subject of increasing scientific attention. While neonatology pushes the definition of viability ever earlier, ultrasound and fetology expand the concept of the patient in utero. Within such a continuous growth process, it is hard to defend logically any demarcation point after conception as the point at which an immature form of human life is so different from the day before or the day after, that it can be morally or legally discounted as a nonperson. Even the moment of birth can hardly differentiate a nine-month fetus from a newborn. It is not surprising that those who countenance late abortions are logically led to endorse selective infanticide.

The same legal tradition which in our society guarantees the right to control one's own body firmly recognizes the wrongfulness of harming other bodies, however immature, dependent, different looking, or powerless. The handicapped, the retarded, and newborns are legally protected from deliberate harm. Pro-life feminists reject the suppositions that would except the unborn from this protection.

After all, debates similar to those about the fetus were once conducted about feminine personhood. Just as women, or blacks, were considered too different, too underdeveloped, too "biological," to have souls or to possess legal rights, so the fetus is now seen as "merely" biological life, subsidiary to a person. A woman was once viewed as incorporated into the "one flesh" of her husband's person; she too was a form of bodily property. In all patriarchal unjust systems, lesser orders of human life are granted rights only when wanted, chosen, or invested with value by the powerful.

Fortunately, in the course of civilization there has been a gradual realization that justice demands the powerless and dependent be protected against the uses of power wielded unilaterally. No human can be treated as a means to an end without consent. The fetus is an immature, dependent form of human life which only needs time and protection to develop. Surely, immaturity and dependence are not crimes.

In an effort to think about the essential requirements of a just society, philosophers like John Rawls recommend imagining yourself in an "original position," in which your position in the society to be created is hidden by a "veil of ignorance." You will have to weigh the possibility that any inequalities inherent in that society's practices may rebound upon you in the worst, as well as in the best, conceivable way. This thought experiment helps ensure justice for all.

Beverly Harrison argues that in such an envisioning of society everyone would institute abortion rights in order to guarantee that if one turned out to be a woman one would have reproductive freedom. But surely in the original position and behind the "veil of ignorance," you would have to contemplate the possibility of being the particular fetus to be aborted. Since everyone has passed through the fetal stage of development, it is false to refuse to imagine oneself in this state when thinking about a potential world in which justice would govern. Would it be just that an embryonic life— in half the cases, of course, a female life—be sacrificed to the right of a woman's control over her own body? A woman may be pregnant without consent and experience a great many penalties, but a fetus killed without consent pays the ultimate penalty.

It does not matter (*The Silent Scream* notwithstanding) whether the fetus being killed is fully conscious or feels pain. We do not sanction killing the innocent if it can be done painlessly or without the victim's awareness. Consciousness becomes important to the abortion debate because it is used as a criterion for "personhood" so often seen as the prerequisite for legal protection. Yet certain philosophers set the standard of personhood so high that half the human race could not meet the criteria during most of their waking hours (let alone their sleeping ones). Sentience, self-consciousness, rational decision-making, social participation? Surely no infant, or child under two, could qualify. Either our idea of person must be expanded or another criterion, such as human life itself, be employed to protect the weak in a just society. Pro-life feminists who defend the fetus empathetically iden-tify with an immature state of growth passed through by themselves, their children, and everyone now alive.

It also seems a travesty of just procedures that a pregnant woman now, in effect, acts as sole judge of her own case, under the most stressful conditions. Yes, one can acknowledge that the pregnant woman will be subject to the potential burdens arising from a pregnancy, but it has never been thought right to have an interested party, especially the more powerful party, decide his or her own case when there may be a conflict of interest. If one considers the matter as a case of a powerful versus a powerless, silenced claimant, the pro-choice feminist argument can rightly be inverted; since hers is the body, hers the risk, and hers the greater burden, then how in fairness can a woman be the sole judge of the fetal right to life?

Human ambivalence, a bias toward self-interest, and emotional stress have always been recognized as endangering judgment. Freud declared that love and hate are so entwined that if instant thoughts could kill, we would all be dead in the bosom of our families. In the case of a woman's involuntary pregnancy, a complex, long-term solution requiring effort and energy has to compete with the immediate solution offered by a morning's visit to an abortion clinic. On the simple, perceptual plane, with imagination and thinking curtailed, the speed, ease, and privacy of abortion, combined with the small size of the embryo, tend to make early abortions seem less morally serious—even though speed, size, technical ease, and the private nature of an act have no moral standing.

As the most recent immigrants from nonpersonhood, feminists have traditionally fought for justice for themselves and the world. Women rally to feminism as a new and better way to live. Rejecting male aggression and destruction, feminists seek alternative, peaceful, ecologically sensitive means to resolve conflicts while respecting human potentiality. It is a chilling inconsistency to see pro-choice feminists demanding continued access to assembly-line, technological methods of fetal killing—the vacuum aspirator, prostaglandins, and dilation and evacuation. It is a betrayal of feminism, which has built the struggle for justice on the bedrock of women's empathy. After all, "maternal thinking" receives its name from a mother's unconditional acceptance and nurture of dependent, immature life. It is difficult to develop concern for women, children, the poor, and the dispossessed— and to care about peace—and at the same time ignore fetal life.

FROM THE NECESSITY OF AUTONOMY AND CHOICE IN RESPONSIBILITY TO AN EXPANDED SENSE OF RESPONSIBILITY

A distorted idea of morality overemphasizes individual autonomy and active choice. Morality has often been viewed too exclusively as a matter of human agency and decisive action. In moral behavior, persons must explicitly choose and aggressively exert their wills to intervene in the natural and social environments. The human will dominates the body, overcomes the given, breaks out of the material limits of nature. Thus if one does not choose to be pregnant or cannot rear a child, who must be given up for adoption, then better to abort the pregnancy. Willing, planning, choosing one's moral commitments through the contracting of one's individual resources becomes the premier model of moral responsibility.

But morality also consists of the good and worthy acceptance of the unexpected events that life presents. Responsiveness and response-ability to things unchosen are also instances of the highest human moral capacity. Morality is not confined to contracted agreements of isolated individuals. Yes, one is obligated by explicit contracts freely initiated, but human beings are also obligated by implicit compacts and involuntary relationships in which persons simply find themselves. To be embedded in a family, a neighborhood, a social system, brings moral obligations which were never entered into with informed consent.

Parent-child relationships are one instance of implicit moral obligations arising by virtue of our being part of the interdependent human community. A woman, involuntarily pregnant, has a moral obligation to the now-existing dependent fetus whether she explicitly consented to its existence or not. No pro-life feminist would dispute the forceful observations of pro-choice feminists about the extreme difficulties that bearing an unwanted child in our society can entail. But the stronger force of the fetal claim presses a woman to accept these burdens; the fetus possesses rights arising from its extreme need and the interdependency and unity of humankind. The woman's moral obligation arises both from her status as a human being embedded in the interdependent human community and her unique lifegiving female reproductive power. To follow the pro-choice feminist ideology of insistent individualistic autonomy and control is to betray a fundamental basis of the moral life.

FROM THE MORAL CLAIM OF THE CONTINGENT
VALUE OF FETAL LIFE TO THE MORAL CLAIM
FOR THE INTRINSIC VALUE OF HUMAN LIFE

The feminist pro-choice position which claims that the value of the fetus is contingent upon the pregnant woman's bestowal—or willed, conscious "construction"—of humanhood is seriously flawed. The inadequacies of this position flow from the erroneous premises (1) that human value and rights can be granted by individual will: (2) that the individual woman's consciousness can exist and operate in an *a priori* isolated fashion; and (3) that "mere" biological, genetic human life has little meaning. Pro-life feminism takes a very different stance to life and nature.

Human life from the beginning to the end of development *has* intrinsic value, which does not depend on meeting the selective criteria or tests set up by powerful others. A fundamental humanist assumption is at stake here. Either we are going to value embodied human life and humanity as good thing, or take some variant of the nihilist position that assumes human life is just one more random occurrence in the universe such that each instance of human life must explicitly be justified to prove itself worthy to continue. When faced with a new life, or an involuntary pregnancy, there is a world of difference in whether one first asks, "Why continue?" or "Why not?" Where is the burden of proof going to rest? The concept of "compulsory pregnancy" is as distorted as labeling life "compulsory aging."

In a sound moral tradition, human rights arise from human needs, and it is the very nature of a right, or valid claim upon another, that it cannot be denied, conditionally delayed, or rescinded by more powerful others at their behest. It seems fallacious to hold that in the case of the fetus it is the pregnant woman alone who gives or removes its right to life and human status solely through her subjective conscious investment or "humanization." Surely no pregnant woman (or any other individual member of the species) has created her own human nature by an individually willed act of consciousness, nor for that matter been able to guarantee her own human rights. An individual woman and the unique individual embryonic life within her can only exist because of their participation in the genetic inheritance of the human species as a whole. Biological life should never be discounted. Membership in the species, or collective human family, is the basis for human solidarity, equality, and natural human rights.

THE MORAL RIGHT OF WOMEN TO FULL SOCIAL EQUALITY FROM A PRO-LIFE FEMINIST PERSPECTIVE

Pro-life feminists and pro-choice feminists are totally agreed on the moral right of women to the full social equality so far denied them. The disagreement between them concerns the definition of the desired goal and the best means to get there. Permissive abortion laws do not bring women reproductive freedom, social equality, sexual fulfillment, or full personal development.

Pragmatic failures of a pro-choice feminist position combined with a lack of moral vision are, in fact, causing disaffection among young women. Middle-aged pro-choice feminists blamed the "big chill" on the general conservative backlash. But they should look rather to their own elitist acceptance of male models of sex and to the sad picture they present of women's lives. Pitting women against their own offspring is not only morally offensive, it is psychologically and politically destructive. Women will never climb to equality and social empowerment over mounds of dead fetuses, numbering now in the millions. As long as most women choose to bear children, they stand to gain from the same constellation of attitudes and institutions that will also protect the fetus in the woman's womb—and they stand to lose from the cultural assumptions that support permissive abortion.

Despite temporary conflicts of interest, feminine and fetal liberation are ultimately one and the same cause.

Women's rights and liberation are pragmatically linked to fetal rights because to obtain true equality, women need (1) more social support and changes in the structure of society, and (2) increased self-confidence, self-expectations, and self-esteem. Society in general, and men in particular, have to provide women more support in rearing the next generation, or our devastating feminization of poverty will continue. But if a woman claims the right to decide by herself whether the fetus becomes a child or not, what does this do to paternal and communal responsibility? Why should men share responsibility for child support or childrearing if they cannot share in what is asserted to be the woman's sole decision? Furthermore, if explicit intentions and consciously accepted contracts are necessary for moral obligations, why should men be held responsible for what *they* do not voluntarily choose to happen? By pro-choice reasoning, a man who does not want to have a child, or whose contraceptive fails, can be exempted from the responsibilities of fatherhood and child support. Traditionally, many men have been laggards in assuming parental responsibility and support for their children; ironically, ready abortion, often advocated as a response to male dereliction, legitimizes male irresponsibility and paves the way for even more male detachment and lack of commitment.

For that matter, why should the state provide a system of day-care or child support, or require workplaces to accommodate women's maternity and the needs of childrearing? Permissive abortion, granted in the name of women's privacy and reproductive freedom, ratifies the view that pregnancies and children are a woman's private individual responsibility. More and more frequently, we hear some version of this old rationalization: if she refuses to get rid of it, it's her problem. A child becomes a product of the individual woman's freely chosen investment, a form of private property resulting from her own cost-benefit calculation. The larger communtiy is relieved of moral responsibility.

With legal abortion freely available, a clear cultural message is given: conception and pregnancy are no longer serious moral matters. With abortion as an acceptable alternative, contraception is not as responsibly used; women take risks, often at the urging of male sexual partners. Repeat abortions increase, with all their psychological and medical repercussions. With more abortion there is more abortion. Behavior shapes thought as well as the other way round. One tends to justify morally what one has done; what becomes commonplace and institutionalized seems harmless. Habituation is a powerful psychological force. Psychologically it is also true that whatever is avoided becomes more threatening; in phobias it is the retreat from anxiety-producing events which reinforces future avoidance. Women begin to see themselves as too weak to cope with involuntary pregnancies. Finally, through the potency of social pressure and the force of inertia, it becomes more and more difficult, in fact almost unthinkable, *not* to use abortion to solve problem pregnancies. Abortion becomes no longer a choice but a "necessity."

But "necessity," beyond the organic failure and death of the body, is a dynamic social construction open to interpretation. The thrust of present feminist pro-choice arguments can only increase the justifiable indications for "necessary" abortion; every unwanted fetal handicap becomes more and more unacceptable. Repeatedly assured that in the name of reproductive freedom, women have a right to specify which pregnancies and which children they will accept, women justify sex selection, and abort unwanted females. Female infanticide, after all, is probably as old a custom as the human species possesses. Indeed, all kinds of selection of the fit and the favored for the good of the family and the tribe have always existed. Selective extinction is no new program.

There are far better goals for feminists to pursue. Pro-life feminists seek to expand and deepen the more communitarian, maternal elements of feminism—and move society from its male-dominated course. First and foremost women have to insist upon a different, woman-centered approach to sex and reproduction. While Margaret Mead stressed the "womb envy" of males in other societies, it has been more or less repressed in our own. In our male-dominated world, what men don't do, doesn't count. Pregnancy, childbirth, and nursing have been characterized as passive, debilitating, animal-like. The disease model of pregnancy and birth has been entrenched. This female disease or impairment, with its attendant "female troubles," naturally handicaps women in the "real" world of hunting, war, and the corporate fast track. Many pro-choice feminists, deliberately childless, adopt the male perspective when they cite the "basic injustice that women have to bear the babies," instead of seeing the injustice in the fact that men cannot. Women's biologically unique capacity and privilege has been denied, despised, and suppressed under male domination; unfortunately, many women have fallen for the phallic fallacy.

Childbirth often appears in pro-choice literature as a painful, traumatic, life-threatening experience. Yet giving birth is accurately seen as an arduous but normal exercise of lifegiving power, a violent and ecstatic peak experience, which men can never know. Ironically, some pro-choice men and women think and talk of pregnancy and childbirth with the same repugnance that ancient ascetics displayed toward orgasms and sexual intecourse. The similarity may not be accidental. The obstetrician Niles Newton, herself a mother, has written of the extended threefold sexuality of women, who can experience orgasm, birth, and nursing as passionate pleasure-giving experiences. All of these are involuntary processes of the female body. Only orgasm, which males share, has been glorified as an involuntary function that is nature's gift; the involuntary feminine processes of childbirth and nursing have been seen as bondage to biology.

Fully accepting our bodies as ourselves, what should women want? I think women will only flourish when there is a feminization of sexuality, very different from the current cultural trend toward masculinizing female sexuality. Women can never have the self-confidence and self-esteem they need to achieve feminist goals in society until a more holistic, feminine model of sexuality becomes the dominant cultural ethos. To say this affirms the view that men and women differ in the domain of sexual functioning, although they are more alike than different in other personality characteristics and competencies. For those of us committed to achieving sexual equality in the culture, it may be hard to accept the fact that sexual differences make it imperative to talk of distinct male and female models of sexuality. But if one wants to change sexual roles, one has to recognize pre-existing conditions. A great deal of evidence is accumulating which points to biological pressures for different male and female sexual functioning.

Males always and everywhere have been more physically aggressive and more likely to fuse sexuality with aggression and dominance. Females may be more variable in their sexuality, but since Masters and Johnson, we know that women have a greater capacity than men for repeated orgasm and a more tenuous path to arousal and orgasmic release. Most obviously, women also have a far greater sociobiological investment in the act of human reproduction. On the whole, women as compared to men possess a sexuality which is more complex, more intense, more extended in time, involving higher investment, risks, and psychosocial involvement.

Considering the differences in sexual functioning, it is not surprising that men and women in the same culture have often constructed different sexual ideals. In Western culture, since the nineteenth century at least, most women have espoused a version of sexual functioning in which sex acts are embedded within deep emotional bonds and secure long-term commitments. Within these committed "pair bonds" males assume parental obligations. In the idealized Victorian version of the Christian sexual ethic, culturally endorsed and maintained by women, the double standard was not countenanced. Men and women did not need to marry to be whole persons, but if they did engage in sexual functioning, they were to be equally chaste, faithful, responsible, loving, and parentally concerned. Many of the most influential women in the nineteenth-century women's movement preached and lived this sexual ethic, often by the side of exemplary feminist men. While the ideal has never been universally obtained, a culturally dominant demand for monogamy, self-control, and emotionally bonded and committed sex works well for women in every stage of their sexual life cycles. When love, chastity, fidelity, and commitment for better or worse are the ascendant cultural prerequisites for sexual functioning, young girls and women expect protection from rape and seduction, adult women justifiably demand male support in childrearing, and older women are more protected from abandonment as their biological attractions wane.

Of course, these feminine sexual ideals always coexisted in competition with another view. A more male-oriented model of erotic or amative sexuality endorses sexual permissiveness without long-term commitment or reproductive focus. Erotic sexuality emphasizes pleasure, play, passion, individual self-expression, and romantic games of courtship and conquest. It is assumed that a variety of partners and sexual experiences are necessary to stimulate romantic passion. This erotic model of the sexual life has often worked satisfactorily for men, both heterosexual and gay, and for certain cultural elites. But for the average woman, it is quite destructive. Women can only play the erotic game successfully when like the *"Cosmopolitan* women," they are young, physically attractive, economically powerful, and fulfilled enough in a career to be willing to sacrifice family life. Abortion is also required. As our society increasingly endorses this male-oriented, permissive view of sexuality, it is all too ready to give women abortion on demand. Abortion helps a woman's body be more like a man's. It has been observed that *Roe* v. *Wade* removed the last defense women possessed against male sexual demands.

Unfortunately, the modern feminist movement made a mistaken move at a critical juncture. Rightly rebelling against patriarchy, unequal education, restricted work opportunities, and women's downtrodden political status, feminists also rejected the nineteenth-century feminine sexual ethic. Amative erotic, permissive sexuality (along with abortion rights) became symbolically indentified with other struggles for social equality in education, work, and politics. This feminist mistake also turned off many potential recruits among women who could not deny the positive dimensions of their own traditional feminine roles, nor their allegiance to the older feminine sexual ethic of love and fidelity.

An ironic situation then arose in which many pro-choice feminists preach their own double standard. In the world of work and career, women are urged to grow up, to display mature self-discipline and self-control; they are told to persevere in long-term commitments, to cope with unexpected obstacles by learning to tough out the inevitable sufferings and setbacks entailed in life and work. But this mature ethic of commitment and self-discipline, recommended as the only way to progress in the world of work and personal achievement, is discounted in the domain of sexuality.

In pro-choice feminism, a permissive, erotic view of sexuality is assumed to be the only option. Sexual intercourse with a variety of partners is seen as "inevitable" from a young age and as a positive growth experience to be managed by access to contraception and abortion. Unfortunately, the pervasive cultural conviction that adolescents, or their elders, cannot exercise sexual self-control, undermines the responsible use of contraception. When a pregnancy occurs, the first abortion is viewed in some pro-choice circles as a *rite de passage*. Responsibly choosing an abortion supposedly ensures that a young woman will take charge of her own life, make her own decisions, and carefully practice contraception. But the social dynamics of a permissive, erotic model of sexuality, coupled with permissive laws, work toward repeat abortions. Instead of being empowered by their abortion choices, young women having abortions are confronting the debilitating reality of *not* bringing a baby into the world; *not* being able to count on a committed male partner; *not* accounting oneself strong enough, or the master of enough resources, to avoid killing the fetus. Young women are hardly going to develop the self-esteem, self-discipline, and self-confidence necessary to confront a male-dominated society through abortion.

The male-oriented sexual orientation has been harmful to women and children. It has helped bring us epidemics of venereal disease, infertility, pornography, sexual abuse, adolescent pregnancy, divorce, displaced older women, and abortion. Will these signals of something amiss stimulate pro-choice feminists to rethink what kind of sex ideal really serves women's best interests? While the erotic model cannot encompass commitment, the committed model can—happily—encompass and encourage romance, passion, and playfulness. In fact, within the security of long-term commitments, women may be more likely to experience sexual pleasure and fulfillment.

The pro-life feminist position is not a return to the old feminine mystique. That espousal of "the eternal feminine" erred by viewing sexuality as so sacred that it cannot be humanly shaped at all. Woman's *whole* nature was supposed to be opposite to man's, necessitating complementary and radically different social roles. Followed to its logical conclusion, such a view presumes that reproductive and sexual experience is necessary for human fulfillment. But as the early feminists insisted, no woman has to marry or engage in sexual intercourse to be fulfilled, nor does a woman have to give birth and raise children to be complete, nor must she stay home and function as an earth mother. But female sexuality does need to be deeply respected as a unique potential and trust. Since most contraceptives and sterilization procedures really do involve only the woman's body rather than destroying new life, they can be an acceptable and responsible moral option.

With sterilization available to accelerate the inevitable natural ending of fertility and childbearing, a woman confronts only a limited number of years in which she exercises her reproductive trust and may have to respond to an unplanned pregnancy. Responsible use of contraception can lower the probabilities even more. Yet abortion is not decreasing. The reason is the current permissive attitude embodied in the law, not the "hard cases" which constitute 3 percent of today's abortions. Since attitudes, the law, and behavior interact, pro-life feminists conclude that unless there is an enforced limitation of abortion, which currently confirms the sexual and social status quo, alternatives will never be developed. For women to get what they need in order to combine childbearing, education, and careers, society has to recognize that female bodies come with wombs. Women and their reproductive power, and the children women have, must be supported in new ways. Another and different round of feminist consciousness-raising is needed in which all of women's potential is accorded respect. This time, instead of humbly buying entrée by conforming to male lifestyles, women will demand that society accommodate to them.

New feminist efforts to rethink the meaning of sexuality, femininity, and reproduction are all the more vital as new techniques for artificial reproduction, surrogate motherhood, and the like present a whole new set of dilemmas. In the long run, the very long run, the abortion debate may be merely the opening round in a series of far-reaching struggles over the role of human sexuality and the ethics of reproduction. Significant changes in the culture, both positive and negative in outcome, may begin as local storms of controversy. We may be at one of those vaguely realized thresholds when we had best come to full attention. What kind of people are we going to be? Pro-life feminists pursue a vision for their sisters, daughters, and granddaughters. Will their great-granddaughters be grateful?

Life in the Tragic Dimension
A Sermon on Abortion

Roger A. Paynter

An old adage says: "There is no fool like an old fool, unless it's a young fool." Being two weeks shy of thirty-seven, I'm not quite ready to say that I am old, but the aches and pains I have after a game of touch football convince me that I am no longer young, either. So, being neither an "old fool" nor a "young fool," I guess I am just foolish—or at least a couple of you have suggested as much to me this week because of my sermon topic this morning. Oh, you haven't actually come out and called me foolish, but you have said, "Why ask for trouble? This is such a volatile issue; there is no way you can win." But, of course, "winning" isn't the issue when you bear the responsibility of standing behind this pulpit, or any pulpit, for that matter. The issue is to try to bring to bear the mercy and love and wisdom of the Gospel on the difficult realities of life. Other reasons also have motivated me to undertake such a difficult task. We have recently, for instance, experienced the anniversary of the Supreme Court's 1973 *Roe v. Wade* decision, which gave women a right to choose with regard to abortion. In addition, the Southern Baptist Christian Life Commission has designated this as "Sanctity of Human Life" Sunday and asked Southern Baptist ministers to address the issue. Those are my reasons for choosing this particular Sunday to address the issue, but I have known, and I mean that in the sense of a conviction, I have *known* that the Gospel of Grace to which I am committed would not allow me forever to avoid this issue in a sermon.

Delivered to the Lake Shore Baptist Church in Waco, Texas, on January 18, 1987. Reprinted by permission of the author.

No issue is more emotionally turbulent at this time as the abortion issue. The sheer amount of published material confirms that. Consequently, no one sermon, no series of sermons for that matter, could begin to take into consideration every dimension of this issue. We could spend weeks dealing only with the Roman Catholic position, or the issue as it relates to poverty, or the difference between a moral and a medical decision, or the relationship of the rights of women to other human rights. If I have learned anything in these last few weeks of preparation, it is that there is simply "too much." There is so much to say, in fact, that I have a very, very hard time imagining how someone can investigate this issue and maintain even the slightest shred of arrogance about the "correctness" of his or her position. Yet people do maintain that, on both sides of the issue.

I have a hard time understanding an attitude of complete confidence because abortion is just about the most extraordinarily complex medical, legal, philosophical, social, and moral issue I have investigated. I want to try to address some of the moral dimensions from a pastoral perspective, and to try to avoid becoming moralistic in the process. In making that effort, I follow this bit of advice from William Sloane Coffin in his sermon on abortion. "Think thoughts that are as clear as possible, but no clearer; say things as simply as possible, but no simpler."[1]

Let me begin with some personal statements. First, I have been in support of the *Roe* v. *Wade* decision. At one point in my life, I took a very liberal stance toward that decision, almost viewing abortion as simply another means of birth control. I hate to cast this in terms of liberal versus conservative, but if one has to, I guess you could say that I have grown more conservative, though I would prefer to say that I have come to a position of understanding the issue from a perspective of more complexity than before. Two things have deeply influenced me in this direction. What little counseling I have done with women and men surrounding the abortion issue has made me aware of its tragic dimension. Second, next Sunday is the fourth birthday of my adopted son, whom I love more than I can possibly say. His birth mother, a seventeen-year-old high school student, faced, I feel sure, the hard issue of whether to abort, and I thank God daily that she did not. Yet, as deeply as I feel about my son, strange as it may sound, I'm glad the young mother had the ability to make a choice—for her sake. So, I am in support of *Roe*. v. *Wade*.

My second personal statement is this: I have come to grieve deeply at the proliferation of abortions—over a million during each of the last few years—because it suggests to me that procreation and abortion decisions are not taken with enough moral seriousness.

The third personal statement I would make is that I find myself incapable of being any kind of absolute moral judge over a woman who makes the painful decision to abort. Yes, men are a part of this issue as well. They do participate in the origin of the fetus, and they also grieve over the difficulty of the decision. But it is essentially an issue confronting the woman, for she is the one who lives intimately with the consequences of her decision. She is the one who has to submit to the medical procedure of abortion. She is the one who, if young, might have to drop out of school, stress her body, and if she so decides, grow up too soon with a baby at her hip. Above all, regardless of age, she is the one who has to make a very complex, morally sensitive decision in a relatively short period of time. With that in mind, I recognize that it may be very difficult for you who are women to hear a man address the issue. (Believe me, I'm probably more in favor of women pastors right now than ever before.)

Now, let me paint the issue in its most extreme ideological perspectives and then muddy the water a bit. These are the expressions that most often get media coverage.

On one extreme is the position that sees the fetus as a piece of human tissue, no more, and the abortion decision as no more a moral choice than removing any other item of mere tissue. This position would say that a woman's right to abortion is absolute. I have read expressions of this position a couple of times, and I have seen it posed in television debates, but I have never known anyone to claim it as *their* position. Each writer or speaker qualifies his or her position in some manner.

The other extreme, the "Right to Life" position, says that from conception the life begun is a human person and to abort a fetus is murder. The fetus's right to life is *absolute*.

Now let me begin to "muddy the waters" by saying that an absolute right—that is, *one* right taken out of the framework of *all other rights*—is often what gets us into trouble. As Abraham Heschel said, "The opposite of a profound truth is another profound truth and the opposite of a human right is another human right."[2]

The first point I would make is that the worlds of medicine, philosophy, and the law have been unable to determine a "magic moment" when personhood begins. Life begins at conception, but when does human personhood begin? A variety of positions have been taken:

(1) *conception,* the point at which the new genotype is set.

(2) *implantation,* when the conceptus implants in the mother's womb (fourteen days). [By the way, the IUD contraceptive device comes into consideration here, for it works not by preventing conception, but by keeping implantation from occurring.]

(3) *eight weeks,* when the cerebral cortex begins to form and all internal organs are formed. Both Aristotle and Augustine believed that a male fetus obtained its soul at forty days and a female fetus was

ensouled at eighty to ninety days. Augustine called this homon-
ization—the point at which a developing embryo experiences
"ensoulment." Before this point (eight weeks), Augustine allowed
for the possibility of abortion. Arguing about the possible resur-
rection of aborted fetuses, "which are fully formed," he says about
those *not* fully formed: "Who is not disposed to think that unformed
fetuses perish like seeds which have been fructified." There is a whole
history of important positions that the early church fathers held
with respect to this issue, a history that the Roman Church would
rather not admit into consideration.[3]

(4) *quickening,* (sixteen to eighteen weeks) when the mother feels the
fetus move.

(5) *viability,* when the unborn child can survive outside the mother's
body (around twenty-six weeks). This is the point when the Supreme
Court protects the life of the unborn. A woman can have an abortion
in the last "trimester" only if her life is at stake.

(6) *birth,* when the baby draws its first breath.

Thousands of years of debate are represented in these positions, and
still there is no consensus about when human life becomes a human person.
Despite the efforts of movies like *The Silent Scream,* no scientific information
can yet determine when unborn life becomes a human person. Just as medical
science has never absolutely, clearly, and without an ounce of reservation
been able to determine when a dying person loses personhood, science cannot
tell us with absolute clarity when personhood begins.

But neither has the church formed a consensus on the question, "When
does personhood begin?" One of the reasons for this lack of consensus is
that the Bible has no clear word. In the absence of such a clear mandate,
a number of interpretations have arisen. Let me share some with you. I
repeat, there is no place in the Bible where it is said: "Thou shalt not have
an abortion."

The primary Jewish position is that human personhood begins when
the baby is born and draws breath. Genesis 2:7 declares that "God breathed
into his nostrils the breath of life and man became a living soul." Elsewhere,
there is a place in Old Testament law (Exodus 21:22–25) that makes a value
distinction between the life of the mother and the life of the unborn:

When men strive together and hurt a woman with child, so that this is
miscarriage, and yet no harm follows, the one who hurt her shall be fined,
according as the woman's husband shall lay upon him . . . if any *harm* follows
then you shall give life for life, eye for eye, tooth for tooth, hand for hand. . . .

That is, if the being *in utero* is harmed, a fine is imposed; if the mother dies, then the life of the injurer is demanded. While this is not the noblest form of jurisprudence, it is the only passage in the Bible directly applicable to the abortion issue. The New Testament, by the way, is completely and strangely silent.[4]

Now, the "Right to Life" people have, as you well know, a number of biblical passages at their disposal—the prominent ones being from Jeremiah, Job, and the Psalmist:

> Before I formed you in the womb, I knew you. (Jeremiah 1:4-5)

> Your own hands shaped me, molded me. (Job 10:8)

> For thou didst form my inward parts—Thou didst knit me together in my mother's womb. (Psalm 139:13)

These passages are all poetic expressions of the truth that God is the Creator and the Source of all creative processes. They should instill in us a reverence toward all life, unborn as well as born. However, I do not think we should use them as proof of when, in the complex physical, spiritual process of creation, fetal life becomes human personhood. Poetry and "legal or scientific" arguments do not mix well. When a man says he has a broken heart, the physician does not do "open-heart" surgery. So I object in principle to the poetry of Genesis 2:7 (God "breathing" into us his breath and making us living souls) being used as a prooftext to defend abortion. And, I object to Psalm 139 (God "knitting" us in our mother's womb) being used as a prooftext to condemn abortion.[5] The poetic language of the Bible is designed to inspire us to respect all life, but it is not designed to determine when fetal life becomes human personality. We are therefore left before the mystery of life with a question mark in our hearts. That leads me to the Scripture that expresses my *knowing* and *unknowing:* "As you do not know how the Spirit comes to the bones in the womb of the mother with child, so you do not know the work of God who makes everything" (Ecclesiastes 11:5).

The Bible does not prohibit abortion, but it always encourages a respect for life. Left with this ambiguity, believers have through the years taken very different positions. The Jewish community, for the most part, has valued the life and health of the mother above that of the unborn.[6] The Roman Catholic Church has held its very clear position only since 1869 and Pope Pius IX. It has always been against the abortion of a human being—don't get me wrong—but thinkers in the Catholic Church have held diverse opinions about when the fetus becomes an ensouled being. A diversity of opinions is still held, but no longer formally. The issue is now covered by the legislative function of the church. Abortions can get you excommunicated. You cannot have an abortion, even to save the life of the mother. You may try to save the mother's life and *indirectly* end the life of the fetus. This is to be contrasted, in Catholic reasoning, from directly aborting the fetus.[7] By the way, the legislative function of the Catholic Church is different from the teaching office, the Magisterium. The pope is infallible only in the teaching, not in the legislative area. Therefore, the prohibition of abortion is not governed by papal infallibility.[8]

Protestant groups have taken a whole range of positions. Southern Baptists have repeatedly gone on record as opposing abortion, except in the case of rape, incest, severe fetal deformity, or danger to the mother's health.[9] Thus, we must invoke the Protestant principle which says that in cases where Scripture is not clear, final interpretation should be left to each individual person, given guidance within his or her community of faith. The Roman Catholic position, of course, is that the church interprets Scripture for all its people on all issues.

Where do we go? Here are some suggestions for your consideration. This may or may not be a word from the Lord; you will have to decide. I offer it to you with fear and trembling, so great is the mystery of life and death at any point on the human spectrum.

(1) Conception is the beginning of life. The Bible teaches respect for all life, so unborn life deserves our deep respect.

(2) We cannot know when a fetus develops human personhood, so I cannot take either extreme position dogmatically. I cannot say that the fetus is just another mass of cells; neither can I say that it is a human person whose life, when we end it, makes us murderers.

(3) Every abortion represents a critical decision and should never be taken as casual birth control.

(4) We must be very careful in even mentioning God's will. We cannot glibly claim God's Will is involved in every conception. I cannot ascribe to God's Will conception by rape or by incest or by a couple in no position to marry and parent a child. These are all occurrences in a tragic and sinful world. Thus, abortion is not the automatic breaking of God's Will. Neither can we glibly say that it is God's Will that we perform abortion. In general, we should say that God is against the ending of all life, but that in some tragic circumstances, He understands—even allows—and certainly forgives the choices we have to make.[10]

(5) Making choices about abortion teaches us how to journey through the tragic dimension of life. This dimension includes violence and poverty, genetic defects, and pregnancy outside marriage. It includes

unwise choices that result in severe and stressful consequences. It includes tragedy that comes when we have done nothing wrong. The tragic dimension of life is when there are no good choices left and everyone loses; when the choices left are not between good and evil, but between the lesser of two evils; or when we painfully, prayerfully, consider what is least bad.[11]

All of us find ourselves in places where no good solution is left. We can only measure the losses and compare the hurt. In such cases, we find ourselves cast out of the innocence of Eden, making choices we hate to make but have to make—with fear and trembling—amid confession and tears.[12]

And the church's role? It is to guide in the decision-making process by doing what I'm doing: safeguarding the woman's freedom of religion to make the choice; to affirm her in her willingness to bear a child under difficult circumstances if that is her choice; and if she decides instead to have an abortion, not to tell her what she should be feeling. Instead:

if she feels guilt—to offer and act out the Grace of God;

if she feels grief—to offer and act out the Comfort of God;

if she feels remorse—to offer and act out the Peace of God;

if she feels fear—to offer and act out the Love of God.

Many, if not most of us, are disturbed by this issue and by the number of abortions. Maybe we can help people make wiser, more educated choices. We have that responsibility. But, life being what it is, abortion decisions will always have to be made—at least until further technology comes along that may preclude it. Since there is no moral consensus or biblical mandate, we should accord women the legal, moral, and religious freedom to choose. And since abortion is a serious moral crisis, we should be around to guide her beforehand and to support and love her through whatever decision she, under God, makes.[13]

This sermon is an interim report, influenced by the thinking of others, and struggled with at a personal level by one who does not have all the answers. It is the best I can do, for now. I say it with apprehension and some sadness. It is as clear as I can think, but no clearer—it is as simple as I can speak, but no simpler. May God have grace and understanding for women who must make such decisions—and for preachers who talk about it.

NOTES

1. William Sloane Coffin, *The Courage to Love* (New York: Harper and Row, 1984), p. 49.

2. Abraham Joshua Heschel, from the original version of his sermon on abortion.

3. Jane Hurst, "The History of Abortion in the Catholic Church: The Untold Story" (Washington, D.C.: Catholics for a Free Choice, 1981), p. 7.

4. H. Stephen Shoemaker, unpublished sermon, "The Moral Crisis of Abortion."

5. Ibid.

6. Rabbi David Feldman as quoted by Paul Simmons, *Birth and Death: Bioethical Decisionmaking* (Philadelphia: Westminster Press, 1983), p. 94.

7. Hurst, p. 17.

8. Ibid., p. 2.

9. Southern Baptist Christian Life Commission pamphlet on abortion, p. 1.

10. Shoemaker.

11. Ibid.

12. William Willimon, *Sighing for Eden* (Nashville: Abingdon Press, 1985), p. 24.

13. Coffin.

Webster v. Reproductive Health Services

In its decision of July 3, 1989, the United States Supreme Court reversed a decision of the United States Court of Appeals for the Eighth Circuit. The Court of Appeals had itself upheld the decision of a Federal District Court.* The case involved a 1986 Missouri law regulating abortion. The preamble to the Missouri statute states that "the life of each human being begins at conception" and that "unborn children have protectable interests in life, health, and well-being." Key provisions of the law (1) prohibit the use of public employees and facilities to perform abortions not necessary to save the life of the mother and (2) specify that the physician, when having reason to believe that the woman is carrying a fetus of at least twenty weeks of gestational age, must adopt procedures necessary to determine the viability of the unborn child. This second provision is the highly controversial section 188.029 of the Missouri law. In the published opinions of the justices, this section is frequently referred to by number. The controversy over section 188.029 concerns the extent to which it mandates medical tests to determine viability of the fetus and the extent to which it modifies the Court's ruling in Roe v. Wade *(1973).*

In the written opinions of the justices, when "court" is written with a lowercase "c," reference is to the District Court or the Eighth Circuit Court of Appeals. When "Court" is written with an uppercase "C," reference is to the Supreme Court.—Eds.

Chief Justice Rehnquist announced the judgment of the Court and delivered the opinion of the Court. . . .

---

*What follows are excerpts of the plurality decision of the Court, in which Chief Justice Rehnquist delivered the judgment of the Court, joined in part by Justices White and Kennedy. Justices O'Connor and Scalia concurred with the judgment and concurred in part with the opinion, while Justices Blackmun, Brennan, Marshall, and Stevens dissented in part. (No. 88–605) Internal reference citations and footnotes have been deleted.—Eds.

151

This appeal concerns the constitutionality of a Missouri statute regulating the performance of abortions. The United States Court of Appeals for the Eighth Circuit struck down several provisions of the statute on the ground that they violated this Court's decision in *Roe* v. *Wade*. . . . We . . . now reverse [the decision of the Court of Appeals].

I

In June 1986, the Governor of Missouri signed into law [an act] . . . which amended existing state law concerning unborn children and abortions. The Act consisted of 20 provisions, 5 of which are now before the Court. The first provision, or preamble, contains "findings" by the state legislature that "[t]he life of each human being begins at conception," and that "unborn children have protectable interests in life, health, and well-being." The Act further requires that all Missouri laws be interpreted to provide unborn children with the same rights enjoyed by other persons, subject to the Federal Constitution and this Court's precedents. Among its other provisions, the Act requires that, prior to performing an abortion on any woman whom a physician has reason to believe is 20 or more weeks pregnant, the physician ascertain whether the fetus is viable by performing "such medical examinations and tests as are necessary to make a finding of the gestational age, weight, and lung maturity of the unborn child" (§ 188.029). The Act also prohibits the use of public employees and facilities to perform or assist abortions not necessary to save the mother's life, and it prohibits the use of public funds, employees, or facilities for the purpose of "encouraging or counseling" a woman to have an abortion not necessary to save her life (§§ 188.205, 188.210, 188.215).

In July 1986, five health professionals employed by the State and two nonprofit corporations brought this class action in the United States District Court for the Western District of Missouri to challenge the constitutionality of the Missouri statute. Plaintiffs, appellees in this Court,* sought declaratory and injunctive relief on the ground that certain statutory provisions violated the First, Fourth, Ninth, and Fourteenth Amendments to the Federal Constitution. They asserted violations of various rights, including the "privacy rights of pregnant women seeking abortions"; the "woman's right to an abortion"; the "righ[t] to privacy in the physician-patient relationship"; the physician's "righ[t] to practice medicine"; the pregnant woman's "right to life due to inherent risks involved in childbirth"; and the woman's right to "receive . . . adequate medical advice and treatment" concerning abortions.

Plaintiffs filed this suit "on their own behalf and on behalf of the entire

---

*Reproductive Health Services—Eds.

class consisting of facilities and Missouri licensed physicians or other health care professionals offering abortion services or pregnancy counseling and on behalf of the entire class of pregnant females seeking abortion services or pregnancy counseling within the State of Missouri." The two nonprofit corporations are Reproductive Health Services, which offers family planning and gynecological services to the public, including abortion services up to 22 weeks "gestational age," and Planned Parenthood of Kansas City, which provides abortion services up to 14 weeks gestational age. The individual plaintiffs are three physicians, one nurse, and a social worker. All are "public employees" at "public facilities" in Missouri, and they are paid for their services with "public funds." . . . The individual plaintiffs, within the scope of their public employment, encourage and counsel pregnant women to have nontherapeutic abortions. Two of the physicians perform abortions. . . . Following a 3-day trial in December 1986, the District Court declared seven provisions of the Act unconstitutional and enjoined their enforcement. . . . The Court of Appeals for the Eighth Circuit affirmed [the judgment of the District Court], with one exception not relevant to this appeal.

II

Decision of this case requires us to address four sections of the Missouri Act: (a) the preamble; (b) the prohibition on the use of public facilities or employees to perform abortions; (c) the prohibition on public funding of abortion counseling; and (d) the requirement that physicians conduct viability tests prior to performing abortions. We address these *seriatim*.

A

The Act's preamble, as noted, sets forth "findings" by the Missouri legislature that "[t]he life of each human being begins at conception," and that "[u]nborn children have protectable intersts in life, health, and well-being" (Missouri Revised Statute §§ 1.205.1[1], [2] [1986]). The Act then mandates that state laws be interpreted to provide unborn children with "all the rights, privileges, and immunities available to other persons, citizens, and residents of this state," subject to the Constitution and this Court's precedents (§ 1.205.2). . . .

The State contends that the preamble itself is precatory and imposes no substantive restrictions on abortions, and that appellees therefore do not have standing to challenge it. Appellees, on the other hand, insist that the preamble is an operative part of the Act intended to guide the interpretation of other provisions of the Act. They maintain, for example, that the preamble's definition of life may prevent physicians in public hospitals from dispensing certain forms of contraceptives, such as the intrauterine device.

In our view, . . . the preamble does not by its terms regulate abortion or any other aspect of appellees' medical practice. The Court has emphasized that *Roe* v. *Wade* "implies no limitation on the authority of a State to make a value judgment favoring childbirth over abortion." The preamble can be read simply to express that sort of value judgment.

We think the extent to which the preamble's language might be used to interpret other state statutes or regulations is something that only the courts of Missouri can definitively decide. . . . It will be time enough for federal courts to address the meaning of the preamble should it be applied to restrict the activities of appellees in some concrete way. Until then, this Court "is not empowered to decide . . . abstract propositions, or to declare, for the government of future cases, principles or rules of law which cannot affect the result as to the thing in issue in the case before it." We therefore need not pass on the constitutionality of the Act's preamble.

B

Section 188.210 provides that "[i]t shall be unlawful for any public employee within the scope of his employment to perform or assist an abortion, not necessary to save the life of the mother," while § 188.215 makes it "unlawful for any public facility to be used for the purpose of performing or assisting an abortion not necessary to save the life of the mother." The Court of Appeals held that these provisions contravened this Court's abortion decisions. We take the contrary view.

As we said earlier this Term in *DeShaney* v. *Winnebago County Dept. of Social Services,* "our cases have recognized that the Due Process Clauses generally confer no affirmative right to governmental aid, even where such aid may be necessary to secure life, liberty, or property interests of which the government itself may not deprive the individual." In *Maher* v. *Roe,* the Court upheld a Connecticut welfare regulation under which Medicaid recipients received payments for medical services related to childbirth, but not for nontherapeutic abortions. The Court rejected the claim that this unequal subsidization of childbirth and abortion was impermissible under *Roe* v. *Wade.* As the Court put it:

> The Connecticut regulation before us is different in kind from the laws invali-
> dated in our previous abortion decisions. The Connecticut regulation places
> no obstacles—absolute or otherwise—in the pregnant woman's path to an
> abortion. An indigent woman who desires an abortion suffers no disadvantage
> as a consequence of Connecticut's decision to fund childbirth; she continues
> as before to dependent on private sources for the service she desires. The State
> may have made childbirth a more attractive alternative, thereby influencing
> the woman's decision, but it has imposed no restriction on access to abortions
> that was not already there. The indigency that may make it difficult—and

in some cases, perhaps, impossible—for some women to have abortions is neither created nor in any way affected by the Connecticut regulation.

Relying on *Maher,* the Court in *Poelker* v. *Doe,* held that the city of St. Louis committed "no constitutional violation . . . in electing, as a policy choice, to provide publicly financed hospital services for childbirth without providing cocresponding services for nontherapeutic abortions."

More recently, in *Harris* v. *McRae,* the Court upheld "the most restrictive version of the Hyde Amendment," which withheld from States federal funds under the Medicaid program to reimburse the costs of abortions, " 'except where the life of the mother would be endangered if the fetus were carried to term.' ". . .

Missouri's refusal to allow public employees to perform abortions in public hospitals leaves a pregnant woman with the same choices as if the State had chosen not to operate any public hospitals at all. The challenged provisions only restrict a woman's ability to obtain an abortion to the extent that she chooses to use a physician affiliated with a public hospital. This circumstance is more easily remedied, and thus considerably less burdensome, than indigency, which "may make it difficult—and in some cases, perhaps, impossible—for some women to have abortions" without public funding. Having held that the State's refusal to fund abortions does not violate *Roe* v. *Wade,* it strains logic to reach a contrary result for the use of public facilities and employees. If the State may "make a value judgment favoring childbirth over abortion and . . . implement that judgment by the allocation of public funds," surely it may do so through the allocation of other public resources, such as hospitals and medical staff.

. . . Nothing in the Constitution requires States to enter or remain in the business of performing abortions. Nor, as appellees suggest, do private physicians and their patients have some kind of constitutional right of access to public facilities for the performance of abortions. . . .

Thus we uphold the Act's restrictions on the use of public employees and facilities for the performance or assistance of nontherapeutic abortions.

C

The Missouri Act contains three provisions relating to "encouraging or counseling a woman to have an abortion not necessary to save her life." Section 188.205 states that no public funds can be used for this purpose; § 188.210 states that public employees cannot, within the scope of their employment, engage in such speech; and § 18.215 forbids such speech in public facilities. The Court of Appeals did not consider § 188.205 separately from §§ 188.210 and 188.215. It held that all three of these provisions were unconstitutionally vague, and that "the ban on using public funds, employees, and facilities to encourage or counsel a woman to have an abortion is an unacceptable infringement of the woman's fourteenth amendment right to chose an abortion after receiving the medical information necessary to exercise the right knowingly and intelligently."

Missouri has chosen only to appeal the Court of Appeals' invalidation of the public funding provision, § 188.205. A threshold question is whether this provision reaches primary conduct, or whether it is simply an instruction to the State's fiscal officers not to allocate funds for abortion counseling. We accept, for purposes of decision, the State's claim that § 188.205 "is not directed at the conduct of any physician or health care provider, private or public," but "is directed solely at those persons responsible for expending public funds." . . .

D

Section 188.029 of the Missouri Act provides:

Before a physician performs an abortion on a woman he has reason to believe is carrying an unborn child of twenty or more weeks gestational age, the physician shall first determine if the unborn child is viable by using and exercising that degree of care, skill, and proficiency commonly exercised by the ordinarily skillful, careful, and prudent physician engaged in similar practice under the same or similar conditions. In making this determination of viability, the physician shall perform or cause to be performed such medical examinations and tests as are necessary to make a finding of the gestational age, weight, and lung maturity of the unborn child and shall enter such findings and determination of viability in the medical record of the mother.

As with the preamble, the parties disagree over the meaning of this statutory provision. The State emphasizes the language of the first sentence, which speaks in terms of the physician's determination of viability being made by the standards of ordinary skill in the medical profession. Appellees stress the language of the second sentence, which prescribes such "tests as are necessary" to make a finding of gestational age, fetal weight, and lung maturity.

The Court of Appeals read § 188.029 as requiring that after 20 weeks "doctors *must* perform tests to find gestational age, fetal weight, and lung maturity." The court indicated that the tests needed to determine fetal weight at 20 weeks are "unreliable and inaccurate" and would add $125 to $250 to the cost of an abortion. It also stated that "amniocentesis, the only method available to determine lung maturity, is contrary to accepted medical practice until 28–30 weeks of gestation, expensive, and imposes significant health risks for both the pregnant woman and the fetus."

We must first determine the meaning of § 188.029 under Missouri law. Our usual practice is to defer to the lower court's construction of a state statute, but we believe the Court of Appeals has "fallen into plain error" in this case. . . .

We think the viability-testing provision makes sense only if the second sentence is read to require only those tests that are useful to making subsidiary findings as to viability. If we construe this provision to require a physician to perform those tests needed to make the three specified findings *in all circumstances,* including when the physician's reasonable professional judgment indicates that the tests would be irrelevant to determining viability or even dangerous to the mother and the fetus, the second sentence of § 188.029 would conflict with the first sentence's *requirement* that a physician apply his reasonable professional skill and judgment. It would also be incongruous to read this provision, especially the word "necessary," to require the performance of tests irrelevant to the expressed statutory purpose of determining viability. It thus seems clear to us that the Court of Appeals' construction of § 188.029 violates well-accepted canons of statutory interpretation used in the Missouri courts. . . .

The viability-testing provision of the Missouri Act is concerned with promoting the State's interest in potential human life rather than in maternal health. Section 188.029 creates what is essentially a presumption of viability at 20 weeks, which the physician must rebut with tests indicating that the fetus is not viable prior to performing an abortion. It also directs the physician's determination as to viability by specifying consideration, if feasible, of gestational age, fetal weight, and lung capacity. The District Court found that "the medical evidence is uncontradicted that a 20-week fetus is *not* viable," and that "23½ to 24 weeks gestation is the earliest point in pregnancy where a reasonable possibility of viability exists." But it also found that there may be a 4-week error in estimating gestational age, which supports testing at 20 weeks.

In *Roe* v. *Wade,* the Court recognized that the State has "important and legitimate" interests in protecting maternal health and in the potentiality of human life. During the second trimester, the State "may, if it chooses, regulate the abortion procedure in ways that are reasonably related to maternal health." After viability, when the State's interest in potential human life was held to become compelling, the State "may, if it chooses, regulate, and even proscribe, abortion except where it is necessary, in appropriate medical judgment, for the preservation of the life or health of the mother."

. . . To the extent that § 188.029 regulates the method for determining viability, it undoubtedly does superimpose state regulation on the medical determination of whether a particular fetus is viable. The Court of Appeals and the District Court thought it unconstitutional for this reason. To the extent that the viability tests increase the cost of what are in fact second-trimester abortions, their validity may also be questioned under *Akron,* where the Court held that a requirement that second trimester abortions must be performed in hospitals was invalid because it substantially increased the expense of those procedures.

We think that the doubt cast upon the Missouri statute by these cases is not so much a flaw in the statute as it is a reflection of the fact that the rigid trimester analysis of the course of a pregnancy enunciated in *Roe* has resulted in subsequent cases like *Colautti* and *Akron* making constitutional law in this area a virtual Procrustean bed. . . .

*Stare decisis** is a cornerstone of our legal system, but it has less power in constitutional cases, where, save for constitutional amendments, this Court is the only body to make needed changes. We have not refrained from reconsideration of a prior construction of the Constitution that has proved "unsound in principle and unworkable in practice." We think the *Roe* trimester framework falls into this category.

In the first place, the rigid *Roe* framework is hardly consistent with the notion of a Constitution cast in general terms, as ours is, and usually speaking in general principles, as our does. The key elements of the *Roe* framework—trimesters and viability—are not found in the text of the Constitution or in any place else one would expect to find a constitutional principle. Since the bounds of the inquiry are essentially indeterminate, the result has been a web of legal rules that have become increasingly intricate, resembling a code of regulations rather than a body of constitutional doctrine. As Justice White has put it, the trimester framework has left this Court to serve as the country's "*ex officio* medical board with powers to approve or disapprove medical and operative practices and standards throughout the United States."

In the second place, we do not see why the State's interest in protecting potential human life should come into existence only at the point of viability, and that there should therefore be a rigid line allowing state regulation after viability but prohibiting it before viability. . . .

The tests that § 188.029 requires the physician to perform are designed to determine viability. The State here has chosen viability as the point at which its interest in potential human life must be safeguarded. See Missouri Revised Statute § 188.030 (1986) "No abortion of a viable unborn child shall be performed unless necessary to preserve the life or health of the woman." It is true that the tests in question increase the expense of abortion, and regulate the discretion of the physician in determining the viability of the fetus. Since the tests will undoubtedly show in many cases that the fetus is not viable, the tests will have been performed for what were in fact second-trimester abortions. But we are satisfied that the requirement of these tests permissibly furthers the State's interest in protecting potential human life, and we therefore believe § 188.029 to be constitutional.

---

*Refers to the judicial principle that prior decisions of the Court should stand, i.e., not be overturned unless warranted on compelling constitutional grounds.—Eds.

. . . The Missouri testing requirement here is reasonably designed to ensure that abortions are not performed where the fetus is viable—an end which all concede is legitimate—and that is sufficient to sustain its constitutionality. . . .

III

Both appellants and the United States as *Amicus Curiae* have urged that we overrule our decision in *Roe* v. *Wade.* The facts of the present case, however, differ from those at issue in *Roe.* Here, Missouri has determined that viability is the point at which its interest in potential human life must be safeguarded. In *Roe,* on the other hand, the Texas statute criminalized the performance of *all* abortions, except when the mother's life was at stake. This case therefore affords us no occasion to revisit the holding of *Roe,* which was that the Texas statute unconstitutionally infringed the right to an abortion derived from the Due Process Clause. To the extent indicated in our opinion, we would modify and narrow *Roe* and succeeding cases.

Because none of the challenged provisions of the Missouri Act properly before us conflict with the Constitution, the judgment of the Court of Appeals is reversed.

Justice O'Connor, concurring in part and concurring in the judgment.

I concur in Parts I, II—A, II—B, and II—C of the Court's opinion.

I

Nothing in the record before us . . . indicates that . . . the preamble to Missouri's abortion regulation statute will affect a woman's decision to have an abortion. Justice Stevens . . . suggests that the preamble may also "interfere[] with contraceptive choices," because certain contraceptive devises act on a female ovum after it has been fertilized by a male sperm. The Missouri Act defines "conception" as "the fertilization of the ovum of a female by a sperm of a male," and invests "unborn children" with "protectable interests in life, health, and well-being," from "the moment of conception. . . ." . . . Similarly, certain *amici* suggest that the Missouri Act's preamble may prohibit the developing technology of *in vitro* fertilization, a technique used to aid couples otherwise unable to bear children in which a number of ova are removed from the woman and fertilized by male sperm. This process often produces excess fertilized ova ("unborn children" under the Missouri Act's definition) that are discarded rather than reinserted into the woman's uterus. It may be correct that the use of postfertilization contraceptive devices is constitutionally protected by *Griswold* and its progeny but, as with a woman's abortion decision, nothing in the record or the opinions below indicates that the preamble will affect a woman's decision to practice contraception. For that matter, nothing in appellees' original complaint . . . [indicates] that appellees sought to enjoin potential violations of *Griswold*. Neither is there any indication of the possibility that the preamble might be applied to prohibit the performance of *in vitro* fertilization. I agree with the Court, therefore, that all of these intimations of unconstitutionality are simply too hypothetical to support the use of declaratory judgment procedures and injunctive remedies in this case. . . .

II

In its interpretation of Missouri's "determination of viability" provision, . . . the plurality has proceeded in a manner unnecessary to deciding the question at hand. I agree with the plurality that it was plain error for the Court of Appeals to interpret the second sentence of Missouri Revised Statute § 188.029 as meaning that "doctors *must* perform tests to find gestational age, fetal weight, and lung maturity." . . .

Unlike the plurality, I do not understand these viability testing requirements to conflict with any of the Court's past decisions concerning state regulation of abortion. Therefore, there is no necessity to accept the State's invitation to reexamine the constitutional validity of *Roe* v. *Wade*. Where there is no need to decide a constitutional question, it is a venerable principle of this Court's adjudicatory processes not to do so for "[t]he Court will not 'anticipte a question of constitutional law in advance of the necessity of deciding it.'" Quite simply, "[i]t is not the habit of the court to decide questions of a constitutional nature unless absolutely necessary to a decision of the case." The Court today has accepted the State's every interpretation of its abortion statute and has upheld, under our existing precedents, every provision of that statute which is properly before us. Precisely for this reason reconsideration of *Roe* falls not into any "good-cause exception" to this "fundamental rule of judicial restraint. . . ." When the constitutional invalidity of a State's abortion statute actually turns on the constitutional validity of *Roe* v. *Wade*, there will be time enough to reexamine *Roe*. And to do so carefully. . . .

Justice Scalia, concurring in part and concurring in the judgment.

I join Parts I, II-A, II-B, and II-C of the opinion of the Chief Justice. As to Part II-D, I share Justice Blackmun's view, that it effectively would overrule *Roe* v. *Wade*. I think that should be done, but would do it more explicitly. Since today we contrive to avoid doing it, and indeed to avoid almost any decision of national import, I need to set forth my reasons, some of which have been well recited in dissents of my colleagues in other cases.

The outcome of today's case will doubtless be heralded as a triumph of judicial statesmanship. It is not that, unless it is statesmanlike needlessly to prolong this Court's self-awarded sovereignty over a field where it has little proper business since the answers to most of the cruel questions posed are political and not juridical—a sovereignty which therefore quite properly, but to the great damage of the Court, makes it the object of the sort of organized public pressure that political institutions in a democracy ought to receive.

Justice O'Connor's assertion that a "fundamental rule of judicial restraint" requires us to avoid reconsidering *Roe,* cannot be taken seriously. By finessing *Roe* we do not, as she suggests, adhere to the strict and venerable rule that we should avoid " 'decid[ing] questions of a constitutional nature.' " We have not disposed of this case on some statutory or procedural ground, but have decided, and could not avoid deciding, whether the Missouri statute meets the requirements of the United States Constitution. The only choice available is whether, in deciding that constitutional question, we should use *Roe* v. *Wade* as the benchmark, or something else. What is involved, therefore, is not the rule of avoiding constitutional issues where possible, but the quite separate principle that we will not " 'formulate a rule of constitutional law broader than is required by the precise facts to which it is to be applied.' " The latter is a sound general principle, but one often departed from when good reason exists. . . .

The Court has often spoken more broadly than needed in precisely the fashion at issue here, announcing a new rule of constitutional law. . . . It would be wrong, in any decision, to ignore the reality that our policy not to "formulate a rule of constitutional law broader than is required by the precise facts" has a frequently applied good-cause exception. But it seems particularly perverse to convert the policy into an absolute in the present case, in order to place beyond reach the inexpressibly "broader-than-was-required-by-the-precise-facts" structure established by *Roe* v. *Wade*.

The real question, then, is whether there are valid reasons to go beyond the most stingy possible holding today. It seems to me there are not only valid but compelling ones. Ordinarily, speaking no more broadly than is absolutely required avoids throwing settled law into confusion; doing so today preserves a chaos that is evident to anyone who can read and count. Alone sufficient to justify a broad holding is the fact that our retaining control through *Roe,* of what I believe to be, and many of our citizens recognize to be, a political issue, continuously distorts the public perception of the role of this Court. We can now look forward to at least another Term with carts full of mail from the public, and streets full of demonstrators, urging us—their unelected and life-tenured judges who have been awarded those extraordinary, undemocratic characteristics precisely in order that we might follow the law despite the popular will—to follow the popular will. Indeed, I expect we can look forward to even more of that than before, given our indecisive decision today. . . .

It was an arguable question today whether § 188.029 of the Missouri law contravened this Court's understanding of *Roe* v. *Wade,* and I would have examined *Roe* rather than examining the contravention. Given the Court's newly contracted abstemiousness, what will it take, one must wonder, to permit us to reach that fundamental question? The result of our vote today is that we will not reconsider that prior opinion, even if most of the Justices think it is wrong, unless we have before us a statute that in fact contradicts it—and even then (under our newly discovered "no-broader-than-necessary" requirement) only minor problematical aspects of *Roe* will be reconsidered, unless one expects State legislatures to adopt provisions whose compliance with *Roe* cannot even be argued with a straight face. It thus appears that the mansion of constitutionalized abortion-law, constructed overnight in *Roe* v. *Wade,* must be disassembled door-jamb by door-jamb, and never entirely brought down, no matter how wrong it may be.

Of the four courses we might have chosen today—to reaffirm *Roe,* to overrule it explicitly, to overrule it *sub silentio,* or to avoid the question— the last is the least responsible. On the question of the constitutionality of § 188.029, I concur in the judgment of the Court and strongly dissent from the manner in which it has been reached.

Justice Blackmun, with whom Justice Brennan and Justice Marshall join, concurring in part and dissenting in part.

Today, *Roe* v. *Wade,* and the fundamental constitutional right of women to decide whether to terminate a pregnancy, survive but are not secure. Although the Court extricates itself from this case without making a single, even incremental, change in the law of abortion, the plurality and Justice Scalia would overrule *Roe* (the first silently, the other explicitly) and would return to the States virtually unfettered authority to control the quintessentially intimate, personal, and life-directing decision whether to carry a fetus to term. Although today, no less than yesterday, the Constitution and the decisions of this Court prohibit a State from enacting laws that inhibit women from the meaningful exercise of that right, a plurality of this Court implicitly invites every state legislature to enact more and more restrictive abortion regulations in order to provoke more and more test cases, in the hope that sometime down the line the Court will return the law of procreative freedom to the severe limitations that generally prevailed in this country before January 22, 1973. Never in my memory has a plurality announced a judgment of this Court that so foments disregard for the law and for our standing decisions.

Nor in my memory has a plurality gone about its business in such a deceptive fashion. At every level of its review, from its effort to read the real meaning out of the Missouri statute, to its intended evisceration of precedents and its deafening silence about the constitutional protections that it would jettison, the plurality obscures the portent of its analysis. With feigned restraint, the plurality announces that its analysis leaves *Roe* "undisturbed," albeit "modif[ied] and narrow[ed]." But this disclaimer is totally meaningless. The plurality opinion is filled with winks, and nods, and knowing glances to those who would do away with *Roe* explicitly, but turns a stone face to anyone in search of what the plurality conceives as the scope of a woman's right under the Due Process Clause to terminate a pregnancy free from the coercive and brooding influence of the State. The simple truth is that *Roe* would not survive the plurality's analysis, and that the plurality provides no substitute for *Roe's* protective umbrella.

I fear for the future. I fear for the liberty and equality of the millions of women who have lived and come of age in the 16 years since *Roe* was decided. I fear for the integrity of, and public esteem for, this Court.

I dissent.

I

. . . Although I . . . am especially disturbed by its misapplication of our past decisions in upholding Missouri's ban on the performance of abortions at "public facilities," the plurality's discussion of these provisions is merely prologue to the consideraiton of the statute's viability-testing requirement, § 188.029—the only section of the Missouri statute that the plurality construes as implicating *Roe* itself. There, tucked away at the end of its opinion, the plurality suggests a radical reversal of the law of abortion; and there, primarily I direct my attention.

In the plurality's view, the viability-testing provision imposes a burden on second-trimester abortions as a way of furthering the State's interest in protecting the potential life of the fetus. Since under the *Roe* framework, the State may not fully regulate abortion in the interest of potential life (as opposed to maternal health) until the third trimester, the plurality finds it necessary, in order to save the Missouri testing provision, to throw out *Roe's* trimester framework. In flat contradiction to *Roe,* the plurality concludes that the State's interest in potential life is compelling before viability, and upholds the testing provision because it "permissibly furthers" that state interest. . . .

Having set up the conflict between § 188.029 and the *Roe* trimester framework, the plurality summarily discards *Roe's* analytic core as "unsound in principle and unworkable in practice.' " . . .

The plurality opinion is far more remarkable for the arguments that it does not advance than for those that it does. The plurality does not even mention, much less join, the true jurisprudential debate underlying this case: whether the Constitution includes an "unenumerated" general right to privacy as recognized in many of our decisions, most notably *Griswold* v.

Connecticut, and *Roe,* and, more specifically, whether and to what extent such a right to privacy extends to matters of childbearing and family life, including abortion. . . .

But rather than arguing that the text of the Constitution makes no mention of the right to privacy, the plurality complains that the critical elements of the *Roe* framework—trimesters and viability—do not appear in the Constitution and are, therefore, somehow inconsistent with a Constitution cast in general terms. Were this a true concern, we would have to abandon most of our constitutional jurisprudence. As the plurality well knows, or should know, the "critical elements" of countless constitutional doctrines nowhere appear in the Constitution's text. . . .

With respect to the *Roe* framework, the general constitutional principle, indeed the fundamental constitutional right, for which it was developed is the right to privacy. . . . It is this general principle, the " 'moral fact that a person belongs to himself and not others nor to society as a whole,' " . . . that is found in the Constitution. The trimester framework simply defines and limits that right to privacy in the abortion context to accommodate, not destroy, a State's legitimate interest in protecting the health of pregnant women and in preserving potential human life. Fashioning such accommodations between individual rights and the legitimate interests of government, establishing benchmarks and standards with which to evaluate the competing claims of individuals and government, lies at the very heart of constitutional adjudication. To the extent that the trimester framework is useful in this enterprise, it is not only consistent with constitutional interpretation, but necessary to the wise and just exercise of this Court's paramount authority to define the scope of constitutional rights.

The plurality next alleges that the result of the trimester framework has "been a web of legal rules that have become increasingly intricate, resembling a code of regulations rather than a body of constitutional doctrine." Again, if this were a true and genuine concern, we would have to abandon vast areas of our constitutional jurisprudence. . . .

Finally, the plurality asserts that the trimester framework cannot stand because the State's interest in potential life is compelling throughout pregnancy, not merely after viability. The opinion contains not one word of rationale for its view of the State's interest. This "it-is-so-because-we-say-so" jurisprudence constitutes nothing other than an attempted exercise of brute force; reason, much less persuasion, has no place.

In answering the plurality's claim that the State's interest in the fetus is uniform and compelling throughout pregnancy, I cannot improve upon what Justice Stevens has written [in *Thornburgh*]:

> I should think it obvious that the State's interest in the protection of an embryo—
> even if that interest is defined as "protecting those who will be citizens" . . . —

increases progressively and dramatically as the organism's capacity to feel pain, to experience pleasure, to survive, and to react to its surroundings increases day by day. The development of a fetus—and pregnancy itself—are not static conditions, and the assertion that the government's interest is static simply ignores this reality. . . . [U]nless the religious view that a fetus is a "person" is adopted . . . there is a fundamental and well-recognized difference between a fetus and a human being; indeed, if there is not such a difference, the permissibility of terminating the life of a fetus could scarcely be left to the will of the state legislatures. And if distinctions may be drawn between a fetus and a human being in terms of the state interest in their protection— even though the fetus represents one of "those who will be citizens"—it seems to me quite odd to argue that distinctions may not also be drawn between the state interest in protecting the freshly fertilized egg and the state interest in protecting the 9-month-gestated, fully sentient fetus on the eve of birth. Recognition of this distinction is supported not only by logic, but also by history and by our shared experiences.

For my own part, I remain convinced, as six other Members of this Court 16 years ago were convinced, that the *Roe* framework, and the viability standard in particular, fairly, sensibly, and effectively functions to safeguard the constitutional liberties of pregnant women while recognizing and accommodating the State's interest in potential human life. The viability line reflects the biological facts and truths of fetal development; it marks that threshold moment prior to which a fetus cannot survive separate from the woman and cannot reasonably and objectively be regarded as a subject of rights or interests distinct from, or paramount to, those of the pregnant woman. At the same time, the viability standard takes account of the undeniable fact that as the fetus evolves into its postnatal form, and as it loses its dependence on the uterine environment, the State's interest in the fetus' potential human life, and in fostering a regard for human life in general, becomes compelling. As a practical matter, because viability follows "quickening"—the point at which a woman feels movement in her womb— and because viability occurs no earlier than 23 weeks gestational age, it establishes an easily applicable standard for regulating abortion while providing a pregnant woman ample time to exercise her fundamental right with her responsible physician to terminate her pregnancy. Although I have stated previously for a majority of this Court that "[c]onstitutional rights do not always have easily ascertainable boundaries," to seek and establish those boundaries remains the special responsibility of this Court. In *Roe,* we discharged that responsibility as logic and science compelled. The plurality today advances not one reasonable argument as to why our judgment in that case was wrong and should be abandoned.

Having contrived an opportunity to reconsider the *Roe* framework, and then having discarded that framework, the plurality finds the testing provision unobjectionable because it "permissibly furthers the State's interest in protecting potential human life." . . .

The "permissibly furthers" standard completely disregards the irreducible minimum of *Roe*: the Court's recognition that a woman has a limited fundamental constitutional right to decide whether to terminate a pregnancy. That right receives no meaningful recognition in the plurality's written opinion. Since, in the plurality's view, the State's interest in potential life is compelling as of the moment of conception, and is therefore served only if abortion is abolished, every hindrance to a woman's ability to obtain an abortion must be "permissible." Indeed, the more severe the hindrance, the more effectively (and permissibly) the State's interest would be furthered. A tax on abortions or a criminal prohibition would both satisfy the plurality's standard. So, for that matter, would a requirement that a pregnant woman memorize and recite today's plurality opinion before seeking an abortion.

The plurality pretends that *Roe* survives, explaining that the facts of this case differ from those in *Roe*: here, Missouri has chosen to assert its interest in potential life only at the point of viability, whereas, in *Roe,* Texas had asserted that interest from the point of conception, criminalizing all abortions, except where the life of the mother was at stake. This, of course, is a distinction without a difference. The plurality repudiates every principle for which *Roe* stands; in good conscience, it cannot possibly believe that *Roe* lies "undisturbed" merely because this case does not call upon the Court to reconsider the Texas statute, or one like it. If the Constitution permits a State to enact any statute that reasonably furthers its interest in potential life, and if that interest arises as of conception, why would the Texas statute fail to pass muster? One suspects that the plurality agrees. It is impossible to read the plurality opinion and especially its final paragraph, without recognizing its implicit invitation to every State to enact more and more restrictive abortion laws, and to assert their interest in potential life as of the moment of conception. All these laws will satisfy the plurality's non-scrutiny, until sometime, a new regime of old dissenters and new appointees will declare what the plurality intends: that *Roe* is no longer good law.

Thus, "not with a bang, but a whimper," the plurality discards a landmark case of the last generation, and casts into darkness the hopes and visions of every woman in this country who had come to believe that the Constitution guaranteed her the right to exercise some control over her unique ability to bear children. The plurality does so either oblivious or insensitive to the fact that millions of women, and their families, have ordered their lives around the right to reproductive choice, and that this right has become vital to the full participation of women in the economic and political walks of American life. The plurality would clear the way once again for government to force upon women the physical labor and specific and direct medical and psychological harms that may accompany carrying a fetus to term. The plurality would clear the way again for the State to conscript a woman's body and to force upon her a "distressful life and future."

The result, as we know from experience, would be that every year hundreds of thousands of women, in desperation, would defy the law, and place their health and safety in the unclean and unsympathetic hands of back-alley abortionists, or they would attempt to perform abortions upon themselves, with disastrous results. Every year, many women, especially poor and minority women, would die or suffer debilitating physical trauma, all in the name of enforced morality or religious dictates or lack of compassion, as it may be.

Of the aspirations and settled understandings of American women, of the inevitable and brutal consequences of what it is doing, the tough-approach plurality utters not a word. This silence is callous. It is also profoundly destructive of the Court as an institution. To overturn a constitutional decision is a rare and grave undertaking. To overturn a constitutional decision that secured a fundamental personal liberty to millions of persons would be unprecedented in our 200 years of constitutional history. Although the doctrine of *stare decisis* applies with somewhat diminished force in constitutional cases generally, even in ordinary constitutional cases "any departure from *stare decisis* demands special justification." This requirement of justification applies with unique force where, as here, the Court's abrogation of precedent would destroy people's firm belief, based on past decisions of this Court, that they possess an unabridgeable right to undertake certain conduct.

As discussed at perhaps too great length above, the plurality makes no serious attempt to carry "the heavy burden of persuading . . . that changes in society or in the law dictate" the abandonment of *Roe* and its numerous progeny, much less the greater burden of explaining the abrogation of a fundamental personal freedom. Instead, the plurality pretends that it leaves *Roe* standing, and refuses even to discuss the real issue underlying this case: whether the Constitution includes an unenumerated right to privacy that encompasses a woman's right to decide whether to terminate a pregnancy. To the extent that the plurality does criticize the *Roe* framework, these criticisms are pure *ipse dixit*.

This comes at a cost. The doctrine of *stare decisis* "permits society to assume that bedrock principles are founded in the law rather than in the proclivities of individuals, and thereby contributes to the integrity of our constitutional system of government, both in appearance and in fact." Today's decision involves the most politically divisive domestic legal issue of our time. By refusing to explain or to justify its proposed revolutionary revision in the law of abortion, and by refusing to abide not only by our precedents, but also by our canons for reconsidering those precedents, the plurality invites charges of cowardice and illegitimacy to our door. I cannot say that these would be undeserved.

For today, at least, the law of abortion stands undisturbed. For today, the women of this Nation still retain the liberty to control their destinies. But the signs are evident and very ominous, and a chill wind blows.

I dissent.

Justice Stevens, concurring in part and dissenting in part.

Having joined Part II-C of the Court's opinion, I shall not comment on § 188.205 of the Missouri statute. With respect to the challenged portions of §§ 188.210 and 188.215, I agree with Justice Blackmun that the record identifies a sufficient number of unconstitutional applications to support the Court of Appeals' judgment invalidating those provisions. The reasons why I would also affirm that court's invalidation of § 188.029, the viability testing provision, and §§ 1.205.1(1)(2) of the preamble, require separate explanation.

It seems to me that in Part II-D of its opinion, the plurality strains to place a construction on § 188.029 that enables it to conclude, "[W]e would modify and narrow *Roe* and succeeding cases." . . . I agree with the Court of Appeals and the District Court that the meaning of the second sentence of § 188.029 is too plain to be ignored. The sentence twice uses the mandatory term "shall," and contains no qualifying language. If it is implicitly limited to tests that are useful in determining viability, it adds nothing to the requirement imposed by the preceding sentence.

My interpretation of the plain language is supported by the structure of the statute as a whole, particularly the preamble, which "finds" that life "begins at conception" and further commands that state laws shall be construed to provide the maximum protection to "the unborn child at every stage of development." I agree with the District Court that "[o]bviously, the purpose of this law is to protect the potential life of the fetus, rather than safeguard maternal health." A literal reading of the statute tends to accomplish that goal. Thus it is not "incongruous" to assume that the Missouri Legislature was trying to protect the potential human life of nonviable fetuses by making the abortion decision more costly. On the contrary, I am satisfied that the Court of Appeals, as well as the District Court, correctly concluded that the Missouri Legislature meant exactly what it said in the second sentence of § 188.029. I am also satisfied, for the reasons stated by Justice Blackmun, that the testing provision is manifestly unconstitutional under *Williams* v. *Lee Optical Co.*, "irrespective of the *Roe* framework." . . .

To the extent that the Missouri statute interferes with contraceptive choices, I have no doubt that it is unconstitutional under the Court's holdings in *Griswold* v. *Connecticut*, *Eisenstadt* v. *Baird*, and *Carey* v. *Population Services International*. . . .

Indeed, I am persuaded that the absence of any secular purpose for the legislative declarations that life begins at conception and that conception occurs at fertilization makes the relevant portion of the preamble invalid under the Establishment Clause of the First Amendment to the Federal Constitution. This conclusion does not, and could not, rest on the fact that the statement happens to coincide with the tenets of certain religions, or on the fact that the legislators who voted to enact it may have been motivated by religious considerations. Rather, it rests on the fact that the preamble, an unequivocal endorsement of a religious tenet of some but by no means all Christian faiths, serves no identifiable secular purpose. That fact alone compels a conclusion that the statute violates the Establishment Clause. . . .

. . . The preamble to the Missouri statute endorses the theological position that there is the same secular interest in preserving the life of a fetus during the first 40 or 80 days of pregnancy as there is after viability— indeed, after the time when the fetus has become a "person" with legal rights protected by the Constitution. To sustain that position as a matter of law, I believe Missouri has the burden of identifying the secular interests that differentiate the first 40 days of pregnancy from the period immediately before or after fertilization when, as *Griswold* and related cases establish, the Constitution allows the use of contraceptive procedures to prevent potential life from developing into full personhood. Focusing our attention on the first several weeks of pregnancy is especially appropriate because that is the period when the vast majority of abortions are actually performed.

As a secular matter, there is an obvious difference between the state interest in protecting the freshly fertilized egg and the state interest in protecting a 9-month-gestated, fully sentient fetus on the eve of birth. There can be no interest in protecting the newly fertilized egg from physical pain or mental anguish, because the capacity for such suffering does not yet exist; respecting a developed fetus, however, that interest is valid. . . .

The State's suggestion that the "finding" in the preamble to its abortion statute is, in effect, an amendment to its tort, property, and criminal law is not persuasive. The Court of Appeals concluded that the preamble "is simply an impermissible state adoption of a theory of when life begins to justify its abortion regulations." . . . .

In my opinion the preamble to the Missouri statute is unconstitutional for two reasons. To the extent that it has substantive impact on the freedom to use contraceptive procedures, it is inconsistent with the central holding in *Griswold.* To the extent that it merely makes "legislative findings without operative effect," as the State argues, it violates the Establishment Clause of the First Amendment. . . .

Contributors

RICHARD SELZER, a surgeon, is a member of the faculty of the Yale School of Medicine.

JUDITH JARVIS THOMSON is professor of philosophy at the Massachusetts Institute of Technology.

MICHAEL TOOLEY has recently been a Senior Fellow in the Research School of Social Sciences of the Australian National University.

PAUL RAMSEY, deceased, was Harrington Spear Paine Professor of Religion at Princeton University.

MARY ANNE WARREN is a member of the Department of Philosophy at San Francisco State University.

JANE ENGLISH, deceased, was a member of the Philosophy Department of the University of North Carolina, Chapel Hill.

HARRY GENSLER is professor of philosophy at Loyola University of Chicago.

CHARLES HARTSHORNE is emeritus professor of philosophy at the University of Texas, Austin.

JOAN C. CALLAHAN is assistant professor of philosophy at the University of Kentucky.

SIDNEY CALLAHAN is associate professor of psychology at Mercy College, Dobbs Ferry, New York.

ROGER PAYNTER is pastor of Lake Shore Baptist Church, Waco, Texas.